A Brief History of Latin and Romance Languages

With Texts, Translations, and Word Lists

Matthew Leigh Embleton

Copyright ©2023 Matthew Leigh Embleton. All rights reserved.

A Brief History of Latin and Romance Languages

Introduction 1
Latin 2
Vulgar Latin 17
Romance Languages 18
Vulgate Bible, 4th Century 22
Appendix Probi, 7th-8th Century 29
Reichenau Glosses, 8th Century 32
Veronese Riddle, 8th-9th Century 71
Commodilla Catacomb, 8th-10th Century 72
Oaths of Strasbourg, 9th Century 73
Canticle of Saint Eulalia, 9th Century 76
Placiti Cassinesi, 10th Century 81
Vida of Jaufre Rudel, 13th Century 83
Vida of Peire d'Alvernhe, 13th Century 87
Vida of Giraut de Bornelh, 13th Century 92
Cantigas de Santa María, 13th Century 97
Cantico Delle Creature, 13th Century 101
English to Old French 107
English to Old Galician-Portuguese 110
English to Old Italian 112
English to Old Occitan 115
Latin to Old French 119
Latin to Old Galician-Portuguese 122
Latin to Old Italian 124
Latin to Old Occitan 127
Old French to English 131
Old Galician-Portuguese to English 135
Old Italian to English 137
Old Occitan to English 140

Cover: Outline of the Roman Empire with overlaid text
Source: Author's design
All other images in this book are in the Public Domain under the Creative Commons License

Acknowledgments

I have long been fascinated by languages and history, and I am very grateful to the special people in my life who have supported and encouraged me in my work. Thank you for believing in me. You know who you are.

I am also grateful to all those who have helped me test the intelligibility of Latin on native speakers of Romance languages: friends and acquaintances past and present, London tourists, and the people of Rome.

Introduction

How many times have you heard someone say 'Latin is a dead language'?

More often than not they are referring to Classical Latin, a formal and literary style of Latin that existed at a finite period of time, accounting for about 30% of the language's timeline as a whole.

Scholars have been retrospectively defining this timeline of literary Latin for the last century and a half, with a little give-and-take and overlap here and there, but generally resembling something like this:

753 BCE	to	75 BCE	Old Latin or Archaic Latin
75 BCE	to	200 CE	Classical Latin
200 CE	to	800 CE	Late Latin
800 CE	to	1300	Medieval Latin
1300	to	1500	Renaissance Latin
1500	to	1900	Neo-Latin
1900	to	present	Contemporary Latin

In previous centuries, education traditionally focused heavily on Classical Latin because of what was written in that time, building on what the Romans had achieved in the same way that the Romans had built on the achievements of the Ancient Greeks.

In the midst of this focus, some Latin teachers even went so far as to tell their students 'There is no such thing as Medieval Latin, there is only *Classical Latin*, and *mistakes*'.

In modern times some of these teachers have since found their way onto social media platforms and Latin interest groups all over the internet, becoming involved in heated debates with Latin enthusiasts about what is correct and incorrect, what should be included and excluded, and what exists and what does not.

Is someone speaking Latin incorrectly if they are not following the style of its golden age like one of Cicero's speeches?

Transposing that same question to English, is someone speaking English incorrectly because they are not following the style of Charles Dickens? or William Shakespeare? or Chaucer? or Beowulf?

Of course not.

These so-called 'mistakes' or 'vulgarisms' are a reflection of how people actually spoke across the Roman world in their day to day lives, and how that changed over time. It was Vulgar Latin that evolved into the Romance Languages, which are spoken around the world to this day.

A dead language is one that no longer has any native speakers, even if the language is still in use. However, Latin is not dead because it lives on in the Romance Languages, which are its continuation.

Latin

When we think of Latin, some of us think of a school motto, an idea for a tattoo, words and phrases used in church, or memories of learning Latin at school, copying down and attempting to memorise grammar tables, and deconstructing passages of Cicero. Where did this ancient language come from? How did it evolve? And how did it become so important?

Latin began as the language of an italic tribe called the Latinii, living in a small territory called Latium at around 1000 BCE.

Distribution of languages in Iron Age Italy

The early form of the Latin alphabet they used was based on that of the Etruscans, the Greeks, the Phoenicians, and ultimately traceable back to Egyptian hieroglyphs.

A	B	C	D	E	F	I	H	I	K	L	M	N	O	P	Q	S	T	Y	X
A	B	C	D	E	F	Z	H	I	K	L	M	N	O	P	Q	R	S	T	V	X

One of the oldests known texts in Old Latin is the Carmen Saliare, the Songs of the Leaping Priests, fragments of rituals believed to have been introduced during the reign of the second king of Rome, Numa Pompilius 715-673 BCE.

The Salian Priests or 'Leaping Priests'
A. Rich, 1883

In 449 BCE the Law of the Twelve Tables was announced as the foundation of the law of the Roman Republic, and was the basis of Roman law for over a thousand years.

The Twelve Tables, unknown engraving

From around 260-75 BCE several generations of authors from Lucius Livius Andronicus to Quintus Cornificius produced works of drama, comedy, history, poetry and satire in Old Latin that would be built upon by the following generations.

Up until a few decades ago, it seemed that to have a grasp of Latin was to be somewhat cultured, or a sign of having had a good education. In Cicero's time the same was true of Ancient Greek. Rome had conquered Greece in 146 BCE, but Greece then conquered Rome with its rich culture.

Marcus Tullius Cicero 106-43 BCE was a Roman statesman, lawyer, scholar and philosopher. By building on the work of translating and using ancient Greek theory and pratice to perfect his style of Latin, Cicero is credited with ushering in the age of Classical Latin. On one hand he used the wealth of Ancient Greek literature as a model, and on the other found a uniquely Roman voice and identity to discuss ideas and concepts that equalled the Ancient Greek tradition.

"Cuiusvis est errare; nullius nisi insipientes, in errore perseverare".

"It is inherent to make a mistake, none except the foolish, persist in error".

A bust of Marcus Tullius Cicero
Prado Gallery, Madrid

In 27 BCE when Rome changed from Republic to Empire, its territory expanded dramatically along with the reach of influence of its culture and language, particularly the language of administration, law, science, and engineering.

During the period known as *Pax Romana* (Roman Peace), under the leadership of good emperors, Nerva, Trajan, Hadrian, Antonius Pius, Lucius Verus, and Marcus Aurelius, from the year 96 to 180 the Roman Empire reached its maximum extent, and literature and the arts flourished with an ever widening range of subjects and styles. Writers of the time continued to look back to Cicero and Classical Latin and try and emulate it.

A Brief History of Latin and Romance Languages

Nerva Trajan Hadrian

Antonius Pius Lucius Verus Marcus Aurelius

A Brief History of Latin and Romance Languages

The Roman Empire at its greatest extent

Pliny the Elder, Celsus, and Scribonius Largus among others, collected and catalogued existing medical knowledge, and Greek writers such as Dioscorides and Galen also wrote in Latin, contributing to the fields of medicine and science.

Pliny the Elder

Celsus

Scribonius Largus

Dioscorides

Galen

Apuleius, Juvenal, Martial, and Petronius among others used philosophy and satire to explore every aspect of life exporing the important questions of the day, and occasionally daring to ask, where are we heading?

Apuleius

Juvenal

Martial

Petronius

With the growth of Christianity in the Roman Empire came the emergence of Christian texts in Latin, including St Jerome's translation of the Bible from Greek and Hebrew completed in 405.

Latinising much of the theological language of Greek it was intended to be elegantly simple and unornamented so that it could be understood by all Latin speakers, and it was adopted by the Roman Catholic Church whose documents and liturgy became known as Ecclesiastical Latin.

Ecclesiastical Latin or Church Latin contains a mixture of Vulgar and Classical Latin, and also Greek and Hebrew words from the original Old and New Testaments. Some words took on meanings more specific to Christian ideas and theology than their wider original meanings, for example the word 'canticle' from the Latin '*cancitulum*', a diminutive of '*cancitum*' meaning a song, in Ecclesiastical Latin would mean a short hymn or prayer taken from biblical or holy text.

A Brief History of Latin and Romance Languages

St. Jerome
by Peter Paul Reubens, c.1625

By the 5th Century, the invasions of Huns in the East and subsequent invasions of Germanic tribes in the west, referred to as the 'Barbarian Invasions', brought about the decline and fall of the Western Roman Empire. In 476 the barbarian soldier and statesman Odoacer deposed the final emperor Romulus Augustulus to become the ruler of the Kingdom of Italy until 493.

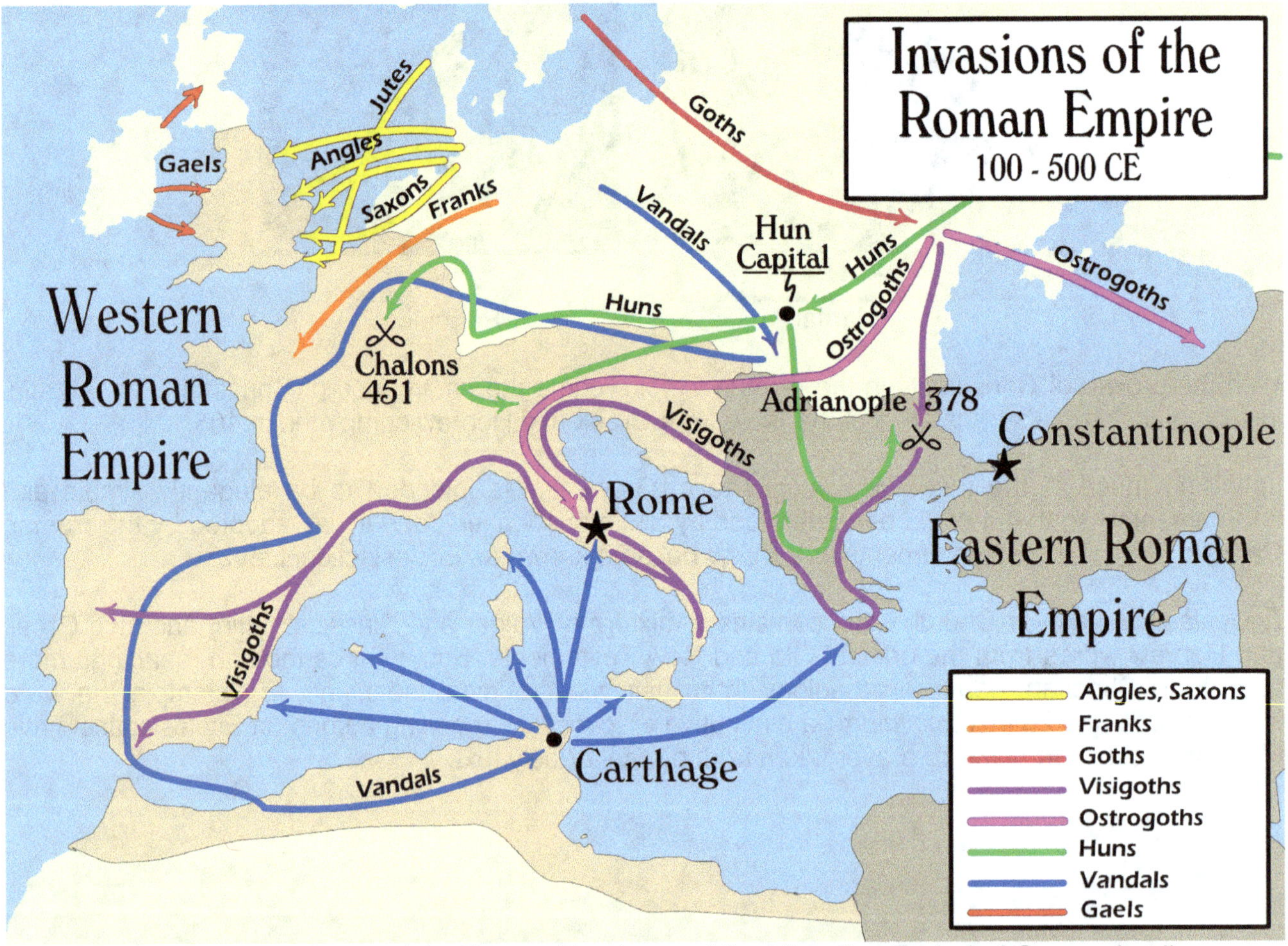

The Barbarian Invasions of the Roman Empire, and the Migration Period of Germanic tribes

A Brief History of Latin and Romance Languages — Latin

The resulting power vacuum brought about what would be called the Migration Period, a large-scale migration of Germanic tribes settlling in former Roman territories, creating a series of successor kingdoms and multiple small states, the so-called Barbarian Kingdoms.

Some of the rulers of these kingdoms had admired the former power and wealth of the Roman Empire, some had served in the Roman Army as mercenaries, and those with ambition wanted to emulate its former success.

The Eastern Roman Empire continued to flourish for nearly another thousand years, centred around its capital in Constantinople (previously Byzantium, from the Greek *Βυζάντιον* = Byzantion). The importance of maintaining the use of Latin in the east was argued by emperors by Diocletian to Justinian the Great, but it was gradually replaced by Greek. Latin remained a minority language in the east, until it evolved into the local eastern romance languages of Dalmation and Romanian.

Over the following centuries in the West, the Franks, a group of Germanic peoples originally from the Lower Rhine area, united and expanded their power and influence to conquer and dominate much of Western Europe, becoming the largest and most powerful state in the West.

The process of adopting Christianiy took place between the 5th and 6th Centuries. First under the Merovingian Dynasty (5th Century until 751), then the Carolingian Dynasty (751 to 800), and later the Carolingian Empire (800 to 888), the Frankish rulers came to see themselves as the inheritors of, or the successors to, the Roman Empire in the West and the defenders of Christianity in the West. This was legitimised by Pope Leo III who crowned Charlemagne on 25th December 800 as a Roman Emperor of an empire which was referred to by various names:

Universum Regnum = The Whole Kingdom
Romanorum sive Francorum Imperium = The Empire of the Romans and Franks
Romanum Imperium = The Roman Empire
Imperium Christianum = The Christian Empire

A denarius of Charlemagne dated c812–814

The inscription reads:

KAROLVS IMP AVG

(Karolus Imperator Augustus)

(Charles the Great Emperor)

Charlemagne brought about a revival of the learning of Latin in the early 9th Century in what was called the Carolingian Renaissance. He invited the leading scholars of the time to his court, including Alcuin of York who wrote a number of educational manuals on grammar, rhetoric, and even Latin pronunciation.

Other literature from this period includes local annals and chronicles, hagiographies (the lives of saints), biographies of other significant people, histories, poetry, travel literature, theological work, and a wide range of legal documents.

The Byzantine Empire at its greatest extent

A Brief History of Latin and Romance Languages — Latin

The Merovingian Kingdoms at their greatest extent

The Carolingian Empire at its greatest extent

A Brief History of Latin and Romance Languages

Medieval Latin developed a much larger vocabulary with many latinised loan words from Greek and Germanic languages, and the style of authors varied increasingly depending on their use of spelling, vocabulary, grammar, and syntax, which often took on that of the author's native language.

Variations in spelling emerged due to frequent abbreviations which were varyingly well known, and differences in the styles of handwriting such as the Carolingian Miniscule.

```
a b c d e f
g h i j k l
m n o p q
r ſ t u x y
```

Carolingian Miniscule Alphabet

For example the letter 't' with a shortened vertical stem resembles the letter 'c' resulting in the word '*etiam*' meaning 'also' appearing as '*eciam*', which can be seen in article 1 of the Magna Carta of 1215.

By the late Medieval Period it became increasingly difficult for those in one country to understand the Latin of another, and even more difficult when attempting to speak or converse. The opinion among the learned Latinists of the time, particularly those in the church, was that Latin was becoming increasingly adulterated and affected by local languages, also including accent and pronunciation.

The massive variation and the quality of Latin came to an end during the rise of nation states and empires, with newly founded universities becoming leading authorities on Latin, imposing a style that was designed to restore the language to its former classical standard. This coincided with the Renaissance Humanism movement, a revival of the study in classical and antiquity. The motto of the movement was '*ad fontes*' meaning 'to the source'. Medieval Latin was perjoratively described by Renaissance humanists as 'gothic' or 'dog Latin', believing instead that only Classical Latin was real Latin.

The plan to revive Latin was successful in education, and schools taught standardised spellings that were written in full without abbreviation, and texts were specially selected for study excluding much of the works from the Late Latin period. While Renaissance Latin was an elegant literary language, it became harder to write about law, medicine, science, or contemporary politics while adhering to these new strict rules, overlooking the original need for latinised loan words in order to be able to discuss ideas and terms that would not have existed in the Classical period.

In the 16th century the invention of the printing press made texts much more widely available, and Latin was the language of choice for authors discussing biology, medicine, zoology, botany, cartography, philosophy, and religion with a pan-European readership.

A Brief History of Latin and Romance Languages　　　　　　　　　　　　　　　　　　　　*Latin*

Coinciding with the Age of Discovery or Age of Exploration, a growing need for increasingly accurate and up to date maps charting newly discovered maritime trade routes and lands brought about a golden age of cartographers in various centres in Europe.

Many of thes maps from this period feature these Latin terms:

accuratissima	most accurate	*meridianus*	meridian
arctici, arcticus	arctic	*mundum*	world
australis	southern	*nova, novum*	new
borealis, septentrionalem	northern	*occidens*	west
carta	chart	*occidentalem*	western
circulus	circle	*oceano, oceanus*	ocean
cognita	known	*orbis*	globe
continens	continent	*oriens*	east
descriptione	desction	*orientalem*	eastern
emendatus	shown	*pars, partium*	part of
geographica	geography	*regiones*	region
glaciale	glacial	*tabula*	intabulation
incognita	unknown	*terra*	land
insula	island	*terrarum*	lands
insulae	islands	*totius, universum*	whole
mare, maris	sea	*tropicus*	tropic

Typis Orbis Terrarum 'Image of the Lands of the World', by Abraham Ortelius, 1570

Sixty percent of English words can be traced back to Latin, and many English speakers could recognise new Latin terms as cognates. In 1597, Francisco Suarez wrote *Disputationes Metaphisicae*, i.e. Disputations of Metaphysics. In 1698, Johan Keppler wrote *Astronomia Nova* i.e. New Astronomy. In 1677, Baruch Spinoza wrote, *Ethica Ordinae Geometrico Demonstrata* i.e. Ethics Demonstrated in Geometric Order. In 1687, Isaac Newton wrote *Philosophiae Naturalis Principia Mathematica* i.e. Natural Philosophy and the Principles of Mathematics.

Francisco Suarez.

Johan Keppler

Baruch Spinoza

Isaac Newton

At the same time, the Protestant Reformation had removed Latin from the liturgies of the churches of northern Europe, which inadvertantly advanced the cause of a new secular Latin rooted in science and education.

Latin was also used as an auxiliary language of diplomacy used in several treaties, such as the peace treaties of Osnabrück and Münster in 1648, and the treaty of Vienna in 1738.

In the early 18th Century, the Hannoverian king George I of Great Britain did not speak English, but communicated in Latin with prime minister Robert Walpole who did not speak German or French.

King George I of Great Britain   Prime Minister Robert Walpole

A classical education became increasingly important in the 18th and 19th centuries, and in the days of the British Empire Latin literature also provided a wealth of texts on military strategy, law, political philosophy and government.

These were seen as instructive for the next generation of students who would grow up to keep the British Empire running, and Latin technical phrases continued to be used in Law.

Sports teams continue to adopt Latin mottos, and sports stadiums across the word echo the architecture of the arenas and hippodromes of the ancient world.

In the United Kingdom for example, various football clubs have Latin mottos:

Arsenal F.C.:	*Victoria Concordia Crescit*	'Victory through harmony'
Everton F.C:	*Nil satis nisi optimum*	'Nothing but the best is good enough'*
Manchester City F.C.:	*Superbia in Proelio*	'Pride in battle'
Queen's Park F.C.:	*Ludere Causa Ludendi*	'To play for the sake of playing'
Sheffield Wednesday F.C.:	*Consilio et Animis*	'by Wisdom and Courage'
Shrewsbury Town F.C:	*Floreat Salopia*	'May Shropshire flourish'
Stoke City F.C.:	*Vis Unita Fortior*	'United Strength is Stronger'
Sunderland A.F.C.:	*Consectatio Excellentiae*	'In pursuit of excellence'
Tottenham Hotspur:	*Audere est Facere*	'To dare is to do'

* a more exact translation of this motto would be 'Not enough unless the best'. The translation here put back into Latin would be more like 'Nil sed optimum bona satis est'.

Some say Latin is a dead language, but it lives on in the languges that are its continuation, and through all that it has influenced and continued to influence.

Vulgar Latin

The highly formal style of literary Latin was not for everyday use, for that there was Vulgar Latin. This was not a separate language, but rather the informal version of Latin.

These days the word vulgar has immediately negative connotations and implies something crude or objectioinable. The original meaning was more like simply 'common' or 'every day'.

The graffiti on the walls of the remains of Pompeii provides evidence of Vulgar Latin, and also some slang words which are indeed vulgar in the modern sense. Even the great champion of Classical Latin Cicero is known to have written letters to his friends using the everyday Latin vulgarisms.

The transition from Classical Latin to Late Latin coincided with a period of destabilisation throughout the Roman Empire referred to as the Crisis of the Third Century, a series of internal conflicts and the decline of centralised power, resulting in less standardisation of Latin acros the sprawling empire. From then on many literary works began to take on the non standard features of Vulgar Latin and the vernacular.

Around the year 300, a document was written in Rome and named after the grammarian Marcus Valerius Probus, becoming known as the Appendix Probi. The document contains a list of 227 common spelling mistakes with their corrections. This sheds light onto how the spelling and pronunciation of Latin had begun to change and evolve steadily towards the Romance languages.

speculum not *speclum*
masculus not *masclus*
articulus not *articlus*

Over the centuries, St. Jerome's translation of the Bible became more and more difficult for novice clergy to read and understand due to local changes in grammar, vocabulary, and pronunciation. At around the 8th Century in the abbey of Corbie in Picardy in northern Frankia, a glossary was created from words of the Bible that had fallen out of use, known as the Reichenau Glossary. It includes words such as 'field', which was '*ager*', but became '*campus*' in modern times the word for the grounds for a university of college. Cheese was originally '*caseum*' but became '*formaticum*' like the Italian '*formaggio*' and the French '*fromage*', 'market' was originally '*forum*' but later became '*mercatum*' like the modern words for forum and market, 'law' was '*juris*' but became '*legis*' like the words jurisdiction and legislation.

In 842 Charles the Bald of West Francia and Louis the German of East Francia swore a pact with Lothair I of Lotharingia, Middle Francia, to recognise Lothair I as the rightful heir of Louis the Pious. Louis the German swore his oath in the Romance Language so that the soldiers of Charles the Bald could understand him. This gives us the first written record of Romance Language as distinct from Latin.

While Vulgar Latin evolved into the Romance Languages, the space between Vernacular and Literary Language widened, there was also a great deal of borrowing of words. Latin was now no longer a native language, but a second language of the educated classes in Medieval Europe. With a degree of patience and cooperation it was still possible for well educated people to speak to each other in Latin if neither spoke each other's native language.

Romance Languages

At the fall of the Western Roman Empire, the Latin speaking world was fragmented, but the Germanic tribes that had invaded Roman Italy, Gaul and Hispania, eventually adopted the Latin language and some elements of Roman culture. But without the standardising influence of centralised administration, regional dialects began to evolve away from each other in different directions becoming the Romance Languages, sometimes referred to as Latin Languages or Neo-Latin languages.

The term 'Romance' comes from the Vulgar Latin and Medieval Latin word '*romanice*' or '*romanicus*' meaning 'in Roman'. The expression '*romanice loqui*' ('to speak in Roman') is distinct from '*latine loqui*' ('to speak Latin'). The English word 'romance' comes from the Middle English '*romauns*' or '*roumance*', from the Anglo-Norman and Old French '*romanz*' or '*romans*', which meant the vernacular language of France as opposed to Latin. The courtly tradition of poems and songs in this language during the Medieval Period often involved knights, heroes, adventures, quests, and contained themes of chivalry, morals, and also love, which is where the modern association of the word comes from.

Romance speaking Europe was a dialect continuum, where local dialects varied only slightly in relation to their neighbours with a high degree of mutual intelligibility. Over longer distances however, those differences increased and accumulated, and the level of mutual intelligibility decreased, until two speakers from either end of the continuum appeared to be speaking different languages. This makes it difficult for linguists to distinguish clear boundaries between dialects and languages for the purposes of classification.

Italian poet, writer and philosopher Dante Alighieri in his Latin essay '*De Vulgari Eloquentia*' ('on the Eloquence of the Vernacular') c1305 tells us of one such linguistic boundary: In the north of France, the affirmative word 'yes' was '*oïl*', from the Latin '**hoc ille*' ('this [is what] he [said]'), hence the area '*Langues d'oïl*'. In the south of France, Monaco, Italy's Occitan Valleys, and Val d'Arn in Catalonia, the affirmative word 'yes' was '*oc*', from the Latin '**hoc*' ('this'), hence the area '*Langues d'oc*'. In Italy (and also Spain, and Portugal), the affirmative word was 'si', from the Latin '*sic*' ('thus'):

> "*Totum vero quod in Europa restat ab istis, tertium tenuit ydioma, licet nunc tripharium videatur;*
>
> *nam alii oc, alii oïl, alii sì affirmando locuntur;*
>
> *ut puta Yspani, Franci et Latini.*
>
> *Signum autem quod ab uno eodemque ydiomate istarum trium gentium progrediantur vulgaria, in promptu est, quia multa per eadem vocabula nominare videntur, ut Deum, celum, amorem, mare, terram, est, vivit, moritur, amat, alia fere omnia*".

"All of Europe that remains from these, there held a third language, but now three varieties can be seen;

For some say 'oc', others 'oïl', and others 'sì' if they speak in the affirmative;

As for example the Spanish, the French, and the Latins.

The sign however that the vernaculars of these three peoples are from one and the same language is apparent, because they have the same words for a lof of what they name, such as 'God', 'heaven', 'love', 'the sea', 'the earth', 'is', 'lives', 'dies', 'loves', and almost all others".

It is also worth noting that Dante refers to the '*si*' affirmative group as '*Latins*' rather than Italians. This is further evidence that the 'Latin' identity had been held on to long after the Western Roman Empire. The Orthodox Church of the Eastern Roman Empire also used the term *Latins* as a synonym for all people who followed Roman Catholic Christianity, generally perjoratively, especially after the schism of 1054 and during the Crusades.

Dante's '*De Vulgari Eloquentia*' continues by searching for the 'illustrious' vernacular among the 14 varieties he has identified in the Italian region, praising the work of poets and particularly the Troubadours of his time, and describing which literary genres are best suited to the vernacular.

A few years later Dante's magnum opus '*La Commedia*' ('The Comedy') later known as '*La Divina Commedia*' ('The Divine Comedy') with its three books '*Inferno*' ('Hell'), '*Purgatorio*' ('Purgtory') and '*Paradiso*' ('Pardise') went on to become one of the greatest works of Italian literature. Dante Alighieri, Giovanni Boccaccio and Francesco Peterarch are often referred to as the fathers of Italian literature, or the fathers of the Italian language. They set the stage for the flourishing of vernacular literature that followed.

Romance languages can be loosely summarised in the following categories:
- Ibero-Romance: Portuguese, Galician, Asturleonese / Mirandese, Spanish, Aragonese, Ladino
- Occitano-Romance: Catalan / Valencian, Occitan (*lenga d'oc*), Gascon (disputed)
- Gallo-Romance: French / Oïl languages, Franco-Provençal (Arpitan)
- Rhaeto-Romance: Romansh, Ladin, Friulian
- Gallo-Italic: Piedmontese, Ligurian, Lombard, Emilian, Romagnol
- Venetan (disputed)
- Italo-Dalmatian: Italian (Tuscan, Corsican, Sassarese, Central Italian), Sicilian / Extreme Southern Italian, Neapolitan / Southern Italian, Dalmatian (extinct in 1898), Istriot
- Eastern Romance: Romanian, Aromanian, Megleno-Romanian, Istro-Romanian
- Sardinian: Campidanese, Logudorese

Today the most widely spoken of the Romance Languages by number of native speakers are Spanish, Portuguese, French, Italian, Romanian, and Catalan.

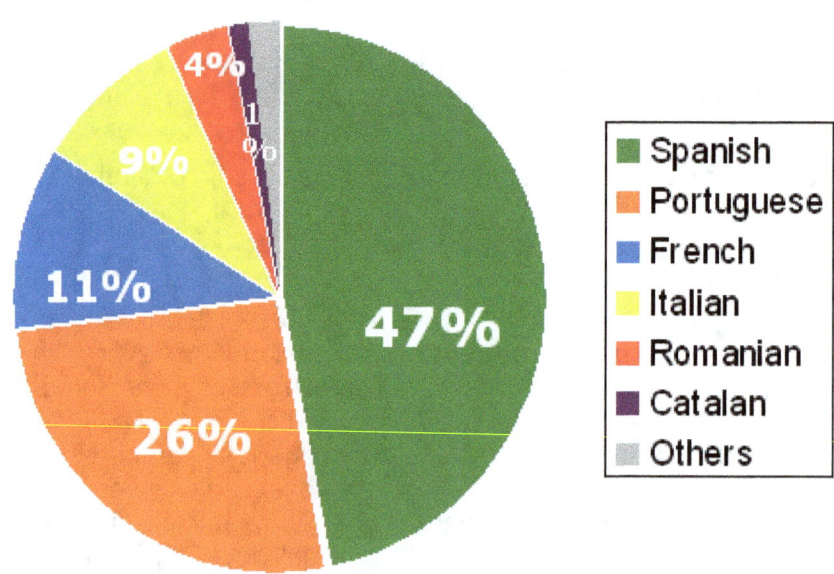

A Brief History of Latin and Romance Languages

Romance Languages

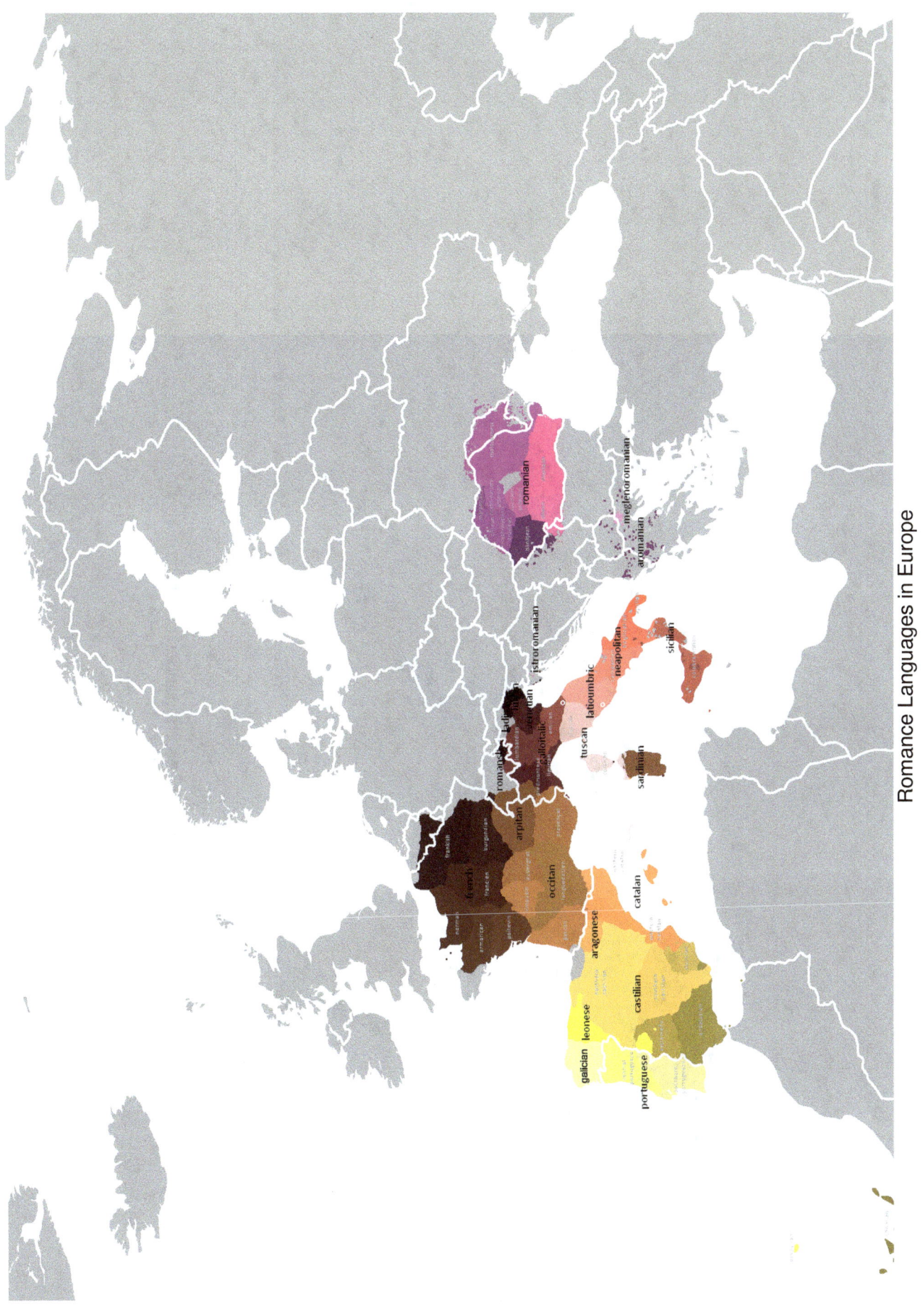

Romance Languages in Europe

A Brief History of Latin and Romance Languages

Romance Languages

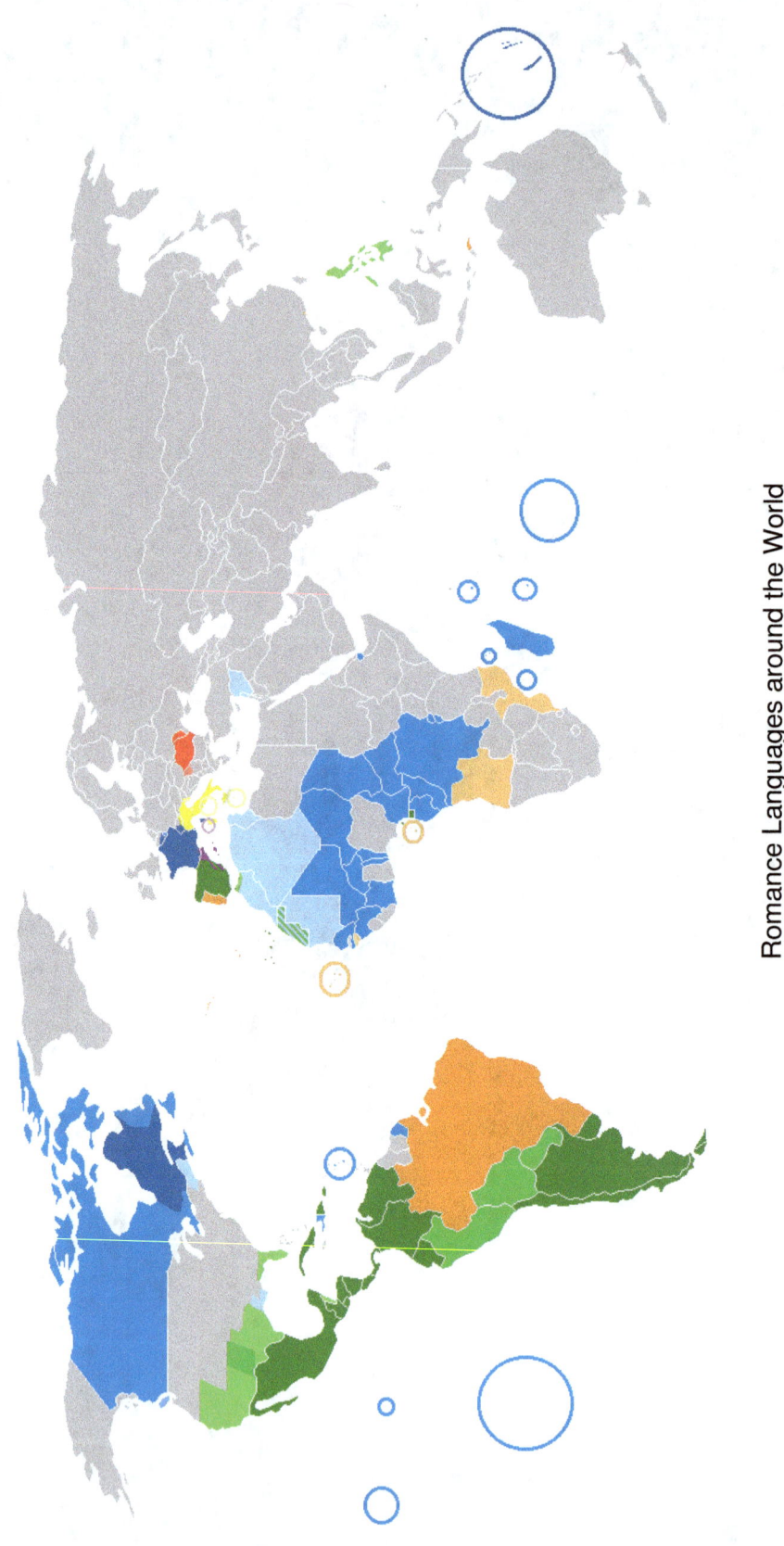

Romance Languages around the World

Vulgate Bible, 4th Century

Latin	Literal	English

Latin

1

Et vidi de mare bestiam ascendentem habentem capita septem et cornua decem et super cornua eius decem diademata et super capita eius nomina blasphemiae.

2

Et bestiam quam vidi similis erat pardo et pedes eius sicut ursi et os eius sicut os leonis.

Et dedit illi draco virtutem suam et potestatem magnam.

3

Et unum de capitibus suis quasi occisum in mortem.

Et plaga mortis eius curata est et admirata est universa terra post bestiam.

4

Et adoraverunt draconem quia dedit potestatem bestiae.

Et adoraverunt bestiam dicentes quis similis bestiae et quis poterit pugnare cum ea.

5

Et datum est ei os loquens magna et blasphemiae et data est illi potestas facere menses quadraginta duo.

Literal

1

And I-saw out-of the-sea a-beast ascending having heads seven and horns ten and on horns each ten crowns and on heads his names of-blasphemy.

2

And the-beast which I-saw similar was a-leopard and feet his as a-bear and mouth his as mouth of-a-lion.

And gave to-him the-dragon strength his and power great.

3

And one of heads his as-it-were slain in death.

And blow of-death his healed it-is and admiration it-is universal the-earth after-the-beast.

4

And they-adored the-dragon which gave power to-the-beast.

And they-adored the-beast saying: who is-similar to-the-beast? and who can fight with him?

5

And given it-is to-him a-mouth speaking great-things and blasphemies and given it-is to-him power to-do months forty two.

English

1

And I saw a beast coming up out the sea, having seven heads and ten horns: and upon his horns, ten diadems: and upon his heads, names of blasphemy.

2

And the beast which I saw was like to a leopard: and his feet were as the feet of a bear, and his mouth as the mouth of a lion.

And the dragon gave him his own strength and great power.

3

And I saw one of his heads as it were slain to death:

and his death's wound was healed. And all the earth was in admiration after the beast.

4

And they adored the dragon which gave power to the beast.

And they adored the beast, saying: Who is like to the beast? And who shall be able to fight with him?

5

And there was given to him a mouth speaking great things and blasphemies: and power was given to him to do, two and forty months.

A Brief History of Latin and Romance Languages   *Vulgate Bible, 4th Century*

Latin	*Literal*	*English*
6	6	6
Et aperuit os suum in blasphemias ad Deum blasphemare nomen eius et tabernaculum eius et eos qui in caelo habitant.	And opened mouth his in blasphemy to God blaspheme name his and tabernacle his and then that in heaven they-live.	And he opened his mouth unto blasphemies against God, to blaspheme his name and his tabernacle and them that dwell in heaven.
7	7	7
Et datum est illi bellum facere cum sanctis et vincere illos.	And given it-is to-him war to-make with saints and overcome them.	And it was given unto him to make war with the saints and to overcome them.
Et data est ei potestas in omnem tribum et populum et linguam et gentem.	And given it-is to-him power in every tribe and people and tongue and nation.	And power was given him over every tribe and people and tongue and nation.
8	8	8
Et adorabunt eum omnes qui inhabitant terram quorum non sunt scripta nomina in libro vitae agni qui occisus est ab origine mundi.	And adored him all that inhabited the-earth whose not they-are written names in the-book of-life of-the-Lamb that was-slain it-is from the-beginning of-the-world.	And all that dwell upon the earth adored him, whose names are not written in the book of life of the Lamb which was slain from the beginning of the world.
9	9	9
Si quis habet aurem audiat.	If who have an-ear let-him-hear.	If any man have an ear, let him hear.
10	10	10
Qui in captivitatem in captivitatem vadit qui in gladio occiderit oportet eum gladio occidi.	That in captivity in to-captivity go that in the-sword killed must he the-sword killed.	He that shall lead into captivity shall go into captivity: he that shall kill by the sword must be killed by the sword.
Hic est patientia et fides sanctorum.	Here it-is the-patience and faith of-the-saints.	Here is the patience and the faith of the saints.
11	11	11
Et vidi aliam bestiam ascendentem de terra et habebat cornua duo similia agni et loquebatur sicut draco.	And I-saw another beast ascending out-of-the-earth and he-had horns two like a-lamb and he-spoke as a-dragon.	And I saw another beast coming up out of the earth: and he had two horns, like a lamb: and he spoke as a dragon.

A Brief History of Latin and Romance Languages *Vulgate Bible, 4th Century*

Latin   Literal   English

12   12   12

Et potestatem prioris bestiae omnem faciebat in conspectu eius. And power of-the-former beast all made in sight his. And he executed all the power of the former beast in his sight.

Et facit terram et inhabitantes in eam adorare bestiam primam cuius curata est plaga mortis. And made the-earth and inhabitants in him adore the-beast the-first whose healed it-is wound death. And he caused the earth and them that dwell therein to adore the first beast, whose wound to death was healed.

13   13   13

Et fecit signa magna ut etiam ignem faceret de caelo descendere in terram in conspectu hominum. And did signs great as also fire he-made from heaven descend in the-earth in in-sight-of men. And he did great signs, so that he made also fire to come down from heaven unto the earth, in the sight of men.

14   14   14

Et seducit habitantes terram propter signa quae data sunt illi facere in conspectu bestiae: dicens habitantibus in terra ut faciant imaginem bestiae quae habet plagam gladii et vixit. And seduced inhabitants of-the-earth because-of-the-signs which-were given they to-him to-do in in-sight-of to-the-beast: saying to-the-inhabitants in the-earth as they-make images of-the-beast which have the-wound by-the-sword and lived. And he seduced them that dwell on the earth, for the signs which were given him to do in the sight of the beast: saying to them that dwell on the earth that they should make the image of the beast which had the wound by the sword and lived.

15   15   15

Et datum est illi ut daret spiritum imagini bestiae ut et loquatur imago bestiae et faciat quicumque non adoraverint imaginem bestiae occidantur. And given it-is to-him as to-give spirit to-the-image of-the-beast as and could-speak the-image to-the-beast and made whosoever not adore the-image to-the-beast should-be-slain. And it was given him to give life to the image of the beast: and that the image of the beast should speak: and should cause that whosoever will not adore the image of the beast should be slain.

16   16   16

Et faciet omnes pusillos et magnos et divites et pauperes et liberos et servos habere caracter in dextera manu aut in frontibus suis. And he-shall-make all little and great and rich and poor and free and bonded to-have a-character on right hand or on forehead theirs. And he shall make all, both little and great, rich and poor, freemen and bondmen, to have a character in their right hand or on their foreheads:

A Brief History of Latin and Romance Languages   Vulgate Bible, 4th Century

17   *17*   *17*

*Et ne quis possit emere aut   And none who might buy or sell   And that no man might buy or
vendere nisi qui habet caracter   unless that had the-character   sell, but he that hath the
nomen bestiae aut numerum   the-name to-the-beast or   character, or the name of the
nominis eius.*   number of-the-name his.   beast, or the number of his
                                                                         name.

18   *18*   *18*

Hic sapientia est.   Here wisdom is.   Here is wisdom.

*qui habet intellectum conputet   that have understanding let-him-   He that hath understanding, let
numerum bestiae.*   count the-number of-the-beast.   him count the number of the
                                                                         beast.

*numerus enim hominis est et   number is of-man it-is and the-   For it is the number of a man:
numerus eius est sescenti   number his it-is six-hundred   and the number of him is six
sexaginta sex.*   sixty six.   hundred sixty-six.

Word List

Latin	English	Latin	English
ab	from	blasphemiae	blasphemies
ad	to	blasphemiae	of-blasphemy
admirata	admiration	blasphemias	blasphemy
adorabunt	adored	caelo	heaven
adorare	adore	capita	heads
adoraverint	adore	capitibus	heads
adoraverunt	they-adored	captivitatem	captivity
agni	a-lamb	captivitatem	to-captivity
agni	of-the-Lamb	caracter	a-character
aliam	another	caracter	the-character
aperuit	opened	conputet	let-him-count
ascendentem	ascending	conspectu	in-sight-of
audiat	let-him-hear	conspectu	sight
aurem	an-ear	cornua	horns
aut	or	cuius	whose
bellum	war	cum	with
bestiae	beast	curata	healed
bestiae	of-the-beast	daret	to-give
bestiae	to-the-beast	data	given
bestiam	a-beast	datum	given
bestiam	beast	de	from
bestiam	the-beast	de	of
blasphemare	blaspheme	de	out-of

A Brief History of Latin and Romance Languages		Vulgate Bible, 4th Century

Latin	English	Latin	English
decem	ten	habentem	having
dedit	gave	habere	to-have
descendere	descend	habet	had
Deum	God (name)	habet	have
dextera	right	habitant	they-live
diademata	crowns	habitantes	inhabitants
dicens	saying	habitantibus	to-the-inhabitants
dicentes	saying	hic	here
divites	rich	hominis	of-man
draco	a-dragon	hominum	men
draco	the-dragon	ignem	fire
draconem	the-dragon	illi	to-him
duo	two	illos	them
ea	him	imaginem	images
eam	him	imaginem	the-image
ei	to-him	imagini	to-the-image
eius	each	imago	the-image
eius	his	in	in
emere	buy	in	on
enim	is	inhabitant	inhabited
eos	then	inhabitantes	inhabitants
erat	was	intellectum	understanding
est	is	leonis	of-a-lion
est	it-is	liberos	free
et	and	libro	the-book
etiam	also	linguam	tongue
eum	he	loquatur	could-speak
eum	him	loquebatur	he-spoke
facere	to-do	loquens	speaking
facere	to-make	magna	great
faceret	he-made	magna	great-things
faciant	they-make	magnam	great
faciat	made	magnos	great
faciebat	made	manu	hand
faciet	he-shall-make	mare	the-sea
facit	made	menses	months
fecit	did	mortem	death
fides	faith	mortis	death
frontibus	forehead	mortis	of-death
gentem	nation	mundi	of-the-world
gladii	by-the-sword	ne	none
gladio	the-sword	nisi	unless
habebat	he-had	nomen	name

A Brief History of Latin and Romance Languages   Vulgate Bible, 4th Century

Latin	English	Latin	English
nomen	the-name	qui	that
nomina	names	quia	which
nominis	of-the-name	quicumque	whosoever
non	not	quis	who
numerum	number	quorum	whose
numerum	the-number	sanctis	saints
numerus	number	sanctorum	of-the-saints
numerus	the-number	sapientia	wisdom
occidantur	should-be-slain	scripta	written
occiderit	killed	seducit	seduced
occidi	killed	septem	seven
occisum	slain	servos	bonded
occisus	was-slain	sescenti	six-hundred
omnem	all	sex	six
omnem	every	sexaginta	sixty
omnes	all	si	if
oportet	must	sicut	as
origine	the-beginning	signa	signs
os	a-mouth	signa	the-signs
os	mouth	similia	like
pardo	a-leopard	similis	is-similar
patientia	the-patience	similis	similar
pauperes	poor	spiritum	spirit
pedes	feet	suam	his
plaga	blow	suis	his
plaga	wound	suis	theirs
plagam	the-wound	sunt	they
populum	people	sunt	they-are
possit	might	super	on
post	after	suum	his
poterit	can	tabernaculum	tabernacle
potestas	power	terra	the-earth
potestatem	power	terram	of-the-earth
primam	the-first	terram	the-earth
prioris	of-the-former	tribum	tribe
propter	because-of	universa	universal
pugnare	fight	unum	one
pusillos	little	ursi	a-bear
quadraginta	forty	ut	as
quae	which	vadit	go
quae	which-were	vendere	sell
quam	which	vidi	I-saw
quasi	as-it-were	vincere	overcome

A Brief History of Latin and Romance Languages   *Vulgate Bible, 4**th** Century*

Latin   English

virtutem   strength
vitae   of-life
vixit   lived

Appendix Probi, 7th-8th Century

Latin	Vulgar Latin	Latin	Vulgar Latin
[catulus	ca<te>llus]	calcostegis	calcosteis
a< >	< >a	calida	calda
acre	acrum	caligo	calligo
adhuc	aduc	camera	cammara
adipes	alipes	cannelam	canianus
Adon	Adonius	capitulum	capiclum
aedes	aedis	Capse[n]sis	Capressis
ales	<alis>	carcer	car<car>
alium	aleum	catulus	catellus
allec	allex	cautes	c<autis>
alveus	albeus	cavea	cavia
amfora	ampora	cithara	citera
amycdala	amiddula	clades	cladis
angulus	anglus	clamis	clamus
ansa	asa	clatri	cracli
anser	ansar	cloaca	cluaca
anser	ansar	cochlea	coclia
anus	anucla	cochleare	cocliarium
aper	aprus	coluber	colober
apes	apis	columna	colomna
aqua	acqua	constabilitus	constab[i]litus
aquaeductus	aquiductus	coquens	cocens
aries	ariex	coqui	coci
articulus	articlus	coqus	cocus
auctor	autor	coruscus	scoriscus
auctoritas	autoritas	crista	crysta
auris	oricla	cultellum	cuntellum
avus	aus	delirus	delerus
baculus	vaclus	deses	desis
balteus	baltius	digitus	dicitus
barbarus	barbar	dimidius	demidius
basilica	bassilica	doleus	dolium
bipennis	bipinnis	draco	dracco
bitumen	butumen	dys<entericus	disinte>ricus
botruus	butro	effeminatus	imfimenatus
brattea	brattia	equs	ecus
bravium	brabium	exequiae	execiae
Byzacenus	Bizacinus	exter	extraneus
caelebs	celeps	facies	fa<ces>
caelebs	celeps	fames	famis
calatus	galatus	faseolus	fassiolus
calceus	calcius	favilla	failla

A Brief History of Latin and Romance Languages   Appendix Probi, 7ᵗʰ-8ᵗʰ Century

Latin	Vulgar Latin	Latin	Vulgar Latin
fax	facla	necne	necnec
Februarius	Febrarius	neptis	nepticla
festuca	fis<tuca>	nescioubi	nesciocobe
figulus	figel	nobiscum	noscum
flagellum	fragellum	noverca	novarca
Flavus	Flaus	noxius	noxeus
formica	furmica	nubes	nubs
formosus	formunsus	numquam	numqua
frigida	fricda	numquit	nimquit
frustum	frustrum	nurus	nura
garrulus	garulus	obstetrix	ops<etris>
glis	<gl>iris	occasio	occansio
glomus	glovus	oculus	oclus
grundio	grunnio	olim	oli
grus	gruis	opobalsamum	ababalsamum
gyrus	girus	orbis	orbs
Hercules	Herculens	orilegium	orolegium
hermeneumata	erminomata	ostium	osteum
hirundo	herundo	palearium	paliarium
hostiae	ostiae	palumbes	palumbus
idem	ide	pancarpus	parcarpus
iecur	iocur	parentalia	parantalia
imago	< >	passer	passar
ip<se>	ip<sus>	passim	passi
iugulus	iuglus	pauper mulier	paupera muli<er>
iunipirus	<iu>niperus	pavor	paor
iuvencus	iuvenclus	pe<rsica>	pessica
labsus	lapsus	pecten	pectinis
lancea	lancia	pegma	peuma
lanius	laneo	plasta	blasta
lilium	lileum	plebes	plevis
linteum	lintium	plebs	pleps
locuples	locuplex	poples	poplex
lues	luis	porphireticum marmor	purpureticum marmur
Marsias	Marsuas	pridem	pride
masculus	mascel	primipilaris	primipilarius
masculus	masclus	proles	prolis
mensa	mesa	puella	poella
meretrix	menetris	pusillus	pisinnus
mergus	mergulus	rabidus	rabiosus
miles	milex	raucus	ra[u]cus
monofagia	monofagium	reses	resis
musium vel musivum	museum	rivus	rius
musivum	mus<e>um	robigo	rubigo
myrta	murta	sedes	sedis

A Brief History of Latin and Romance Languages   *Appendix Probi, 7th-8th Century*

Latin	*Vulgar Latin*	*Latin*	*Vulgar Latin*
senatus	sinatus	vinea	vinia
septizonium	septidonium	vir	vyr
sibilus	sifilus	virga	vyrga
Sirena	Serena	virgo	vyrgo
sobrius	suber	viridis	virdis
socrus	socra	vitulus	viclus
solea	solia	vobiscum	voscum
speculum	speclum	vulpes	vulpis
stabulum	stablum	zizipu\<s\>	zizup\<u\>s
strofa	stropa		
suboles	subolis		
suppellex	superlex		
Syrtes	Syrtis		
tabes	tavis		
tabula	tabla		
terebra	telebra		
terraemotus	terrimotium		
tersus	tertus		
teter	tetrus		
Theophilus	Izophilus		
tinea	ti\<nia\>		
tintinaculum	tintinabulum		
tolerabilis	toleravilis		
tolonium	toloneum		
tondeo	detundo		
tonitru	tonotru		
tribula	tribla		
triclinium	triclinu		
tristis	tristus		
turma	torma		
turma	torma		
tymum	tumum		
umbilicus	imbilicus		
vacua	vaqua		
vacui	vaqui		
vapulo	baplo		
vates	vatis		
vepres	vepris		
vernaculus	vernaclus		
vetulus	veclus		
vico capitis Africae	vico caput Africae		
vico castrorum	vico castrae		
vico strobili	vico trobili		
vico tabuli proconsolis	vico tabulu proconsulis		

Reichenau Glosses, 8th Century

4th Century Word   *8th Century Replacement*

abdito "hidden"   **absconso** "hidden"
                               Old French: escons
                               Old Occitan: escos
                               Catalan: escòs
                               Old Spanish: escuso
                               Old Portuguese: escuso
                               Venetian: sconto
                               Italian: ascoso
                               Romanian: ascuns

abio "go away"   **uado** "hurry, rush"
                               Old French: vois
                               French: vais
                               Catalan: vaig
                               Occitan: vau
                               Spanish: voy
                               Asturian: vo
                               Portuguese: vou
                               Venetian: vago
                               Vegliote: vis
                               Italian: vado
                               Neapolitan: vaco

abgetarii "woodworkers"   **carpentarii** "wagon makers"
                               Old French: charpentier
                               French: charpentiers
                               Occitan: carpentièrs
                               Spanish: carpinteros
                               Portuguese: carpinteiros

absintio "wormwood"   **aloxino**
Old French: assenz   French: aluine
Old Occitan: aussen   Old Spanish: alosna
Spanish: axenxo   Portuguese: alosna
Vegliote: ascianz
Old Italian: assenzo

adolescentia "youth"   **iuuentus**
                               Old French: jovent
                               Occitan: jovent
                               Catalan: jovent

aculeus "stinger"   **aculeonis**
                               French: aiguillon
                               Occitan: agulhon
                               Spanish: aguijón
                               Galician: aguillón

A Brief History of Latin and Romance Languages Reichenau Glosses, 8th Century

4th Century Word   8th Century Replacement

aes   "bronze"   **eramen**
                                       French: airain
                                       Occitan: aram
                                       Catalan: aram
                                       Portuguese: arame
                                       Romansh: arom
                                       Italian: rame
                                       Romanian: aramă
                                       Sardinian (Nuorese): ràmene
                                       Spanish: alambre

ager   "field"   **campus**
                 Occitan: agre   Old French: chans
                 Piedmontese: aire   French: champ
                 Italian: agro   Occitan: camp
                 Romanian: agru 'field, land"   Catalan: camp
                                       Spanish: campo
                                       Portuguese: campo
                                       Romansh: champ
                                       Vegliote: cuomp
                                       Italian: campo
                                       Neapolitan: campo
                                       Sardinian (Nuorese): campo
                                       Romanian: câmp

annuant   "nod"   **cinnant**
                                       Old French: cenent
                                       Old Occitan: cenan
                                       Portuguese: acenam
                                       Italian: accennano

anxiaretur   "worry"   **angustiaretur** "tribulations, difficulties"
                 Old Italian: ansia   French: angoisse
                 Spanish: ansia   Occitan: angoissa
                 Portuguese: ansia 'eagerly await"   Catalan: angoixa

                                       Italian: angoscia

aper   "boar"   **saluaticus porcus**

                 Sardinian: porcapru   Old French: pors salvadges
                                       French: porc sauvage
                                       Occitan: pòrc salvatge
                                       Catalan: porc salvatge
                                       Romansh: portg selvadi
                                       Vegliote: puarc salvutic
                                       Italian: porco salvatico
                                       Romanian: porc sălbatic

arbusta   "orchards"   **arbricellus**   *arboriscellus

A Brief History of Latin and Romance Languages *Reichenau Glosses, 8th Century*

4th Century Word *8th Century Replacement*

	Galician: albustre		*French: arbrisseau*
			Occitan: arbrissèl 'shrubbery'
			Italian: arboscello 'sapling'
area	"threshing-floor"	**danea**	
	French: aire		*Walloon: dègne*
	Occitan: ièra		
	Catalan: era		
	Spanish: era		
	Portuguese: eira		
	Italian: aia		
	Romanian: arie		
arena	"sand"	**sabulo**	"gravel"
	Old French: areine		*French: sablon*
	Occitan: arena		*Occitan: sablon*
	Catalan: arena		*Catalan: sauló*
	Spanish: arena		*Spanish: sablón*
	Portuguese: areia		*Romansh: sablun*
	Italian: rena		*Vegliote: salbaun*
	Neapolitan: rena		*Italian: sabbione*
	Sardinian: rena		*Istro-Romanian: salbun*
	Aromanian: arinã		
armilla	"bracelet"	**baucus**	
	Spanish: armella		*Old French: bou*
atram	"black"	**nigram**	
			French: noire
			Gascon: nera
			Occitan: negra
			Catalan: negra
			Spanish: negra
			Portuguese: negra
			Piedmontese: neira
			Romansh: naire
			Vegliote: niara
			Italian: nera
			Neapolitan: neura
			Romanian: neagră
axis	"axle"	**ascialis**	**axialis*
	French: ais 'plank"		*Old French: aissel*
	Occitan: ais		*French: essieu*
	Catalan: eix		
	Spanish: eje		
	Asturian: eis		
	Portuguese: eixo		
	Italian: asse 'beam, axle"		
benignitate	"kindness"	**bonitate**	

A Brief History of Latin and Romance Languages   Reichenau Glosses, 8th Century

4th Century Word   8th Century Replacement

			French: bonté
			Occitan: bontat
			Catalan: bontat
			Spanish: bondad
			Portuguese: bondade
			Old Italian: bontade
			Italian: bontà
			Romanian: bunătate
binas	"in pairs"	**duas et duas**	
			French: deux à deux
			Spanish: de dos en dos
			Portuguese: de dois em dois
			Italian: due a due
calamus	"reed-pen"	**penna**	"feather, writing implement"
	French: chaume 'stubble, thatch"		Old French: pene
			Portuguese: pena
			Italian: penna
			Sicilian: pinna
			Romanian: peană
callidior	"devious"	**uitiosior**	"wicked", "corrupt"
			Old French: voisos
			Occitan: viciós
			Catalan: viciós 'depraved'
			Italian: vezzoso 'charming'
calumpniam	"slander"	**contentio**	"quarrel, dispute"
	Old French: chalonge		Old Occitan: tensón
	Old Occitan: calonja		
	Old Spanish: caloña		
	Portuguese: coima		
calx	"heel"	**calcaneum**	
	Portuguese: couce		Old French: calcain
	Galician: couce		Gascon: caucanh
	Portuguese: coice		Catalan: calcani
	Old Spanish: coçe		Old Spanish: calanno
	Spanish: coz 'kick'		Romansh: chalchagn
			Italian: calcagno
			Sardinian (Nuorese): carcanzu
			Aromanian: cãlcãnju
			Romanian: călcâi
caminum	"furnace"	**clibanum**	
	Romansh: chamin		
	Vegliote: camain		
	Italian: camino		
cartallo	"basket"	**panario**	"breadbasket"

A Brief History of Latin and Romance Languages   *Reichenau Glosses, 8th Century*

4th Century Word   8th Century Replacement

			French: panier
			Occitan: panièr
			Spanish: panero
			Portuguese: paneiro
			Old Italian: panaio
			Neapolitan: panaro
caseum	"cheese"	**formaticum**	
	Spanish: queso		*French: fromage*
	Portuguese: queijo		*Occitan: formatge*
	Vegliote: chis		*Catalan: formatge*
	Tuscan: cascio		
	Neapolitan: caso		
	Sardinian: casu		
	Romanian: caş		
	Romansh: chaschöl		
crastro	"barracks"	**heribergo**	
	Spanish: castro		*Old French: herberge*
	Portuguese: castro		*Occitan: albèrgo*
cementarii	"stonecutters"	**mationes**	
	French: cimentiers		*French: maçons*
cementariis	"stonecutters"	**macionibus**	
			Occitan: maçons
cenacula	"chambers"	**mansiunculas**	"lodging"
			French: maisons
			Occitan: maisons
			Spanish: mesónes
			Old Portuguese: meijãoes
			Vegliote: mošune 'barns'
			Italian: magioni 'houses'
			Sardinian (Nuorese): masones 'herds'
cesis	"beaten"	**flagellatis**	whipped
			Old French: flaelez
cibaria	"food"	**cibus uiuendi**	"uiuenda" ('that which is necessary for life')
			French: viande 'meat'
			Occitan: vianda
			Italian: vivanda 'food'
			Spanish: vivienda
			Portuguese: vivenda 'residence, housing'
clibanus	"oven"	**furnus**	
			French: four
			Occitan: forn
			Catalan: forn
			Aragonese: furno

A Brief History of Latin and Romance Languages   Reichenau Glosses, 8th Century

4th Century Word   8th Century Replacement

4th Century Word		8th Century Replacement	
			Spanish: horno
			Portuguese: fornu
			Romansh: furn
			Italian: forno
			Neapolitan: fuorno
			Sardinian (Nuorese): furru
			Aromanian: furnu
cliuium	"hill"	*montania*	
			French: montagne
			Occitan: montanha
			Catalan: muntanya
			Spanish: montaña
			Portuguese: montanha
			Romansh: muntogna
			Italian: montagna
			Neapolitan: muntagna
coccinus	"scarlet"	*rubeus*	"red"
			Old French: roges
			French: rouge
			Gascon: arrui
			Occitan: roge
			Catalan: roig
			Aragonese: roio
			Spanish: rubio
			Portuguese: ruivo
			Piedmontese: rubi
			Italian: robbio
			Sardinian (Nuorese): rubiu
			Romanian: roib
colliridam	"pastry"	*turtam*	
			French: tourte
			Occitan: torta
			Spanish: torta
			Romansh: turta
			Vegliote: turta
			Italian: torta
			Sardinian (Nuorese): turta
			Romanian: turtă
commutatione	"exchange"	*concambiis*	
			French: change
			Occitan: cambi
			Catalan: canvi
			Spanish: cambio
			Portuguese: cambio

A Brief History of Latin and Romance Languages　　　*Reichenau Glosses, 8th Century*

4th Century Word　　　　　　　　　　8th Century Replacement

			Italian: cambio
			Romanian: schimb
compellit	"urge"	**anetset**	
			Old French: anecet
			Old Italian: anizza
			Old Portuguese: anaça
concidit	"cut"	**taliauit**	
			French: tailla
			Catalan: tallà
			Spanish: tajó
			Portuguese: talhou
			Italian: tagliò
			Romanian: tăie
contumeliam	"belittlement"	**uerecundiam**	"shame, disgrace"
			French: vergogne
			Occitan: vergonha
			Catalan: vergonya
			Old Spanish: verguenna
			Asturian: vergoña
			Portuguese: vergonha
			Italian: vergogna
			Neapolitan: vregogna
			Occitan: vergunja
			Spanish: vergüenza
			Old Portuguese: vergonça
			Lombard (Milanese): vargonja
			Sardinian (Nuorese): brigunza
coturnices	"quail"	**quacoles**	
	Spanish: codornizes		*French: cailles*
	Portuguese: codornizes		*Occitan: calhas*
	Old Italian: cotornici		*Catalan: guatles*
	Romanian: potârnichi		*Ribagorçan: guallas*
	'partridges"		
			Romansh: quacras
			Italian: quaglie
scabrones	"hornets"	**uuapces**	
	Portuguese: cambrãos		*French: guêpes*
	Italian: calabroni		
crebro	"sieve"	**criuolo**	
			French: crible
			Aragonese: gribafem
			Spanish: cribo
			Portuguese: crivo
			Piedmontese: cribi
			Lombard (Milanese): cribi

A Brief History of Latin and Romance Languages   Reichenau Glosses, 8th Century

4th Century Word   8th Century Replacement

			Sardinian (Nuorese): chilibru
			Romanian: ciur
			Gascon: crièth
			Occitan: crivèl
			Catalan: garbell
			Italian: crivello
crura	"shins"	**tibia**	
			French: tige 'stem'
culmen	"peak"	**spicus**	
	Italian: colmo		French: épi
	Portuguese: cume		Occitan: espic
	Romanian: culme		Friulian: spi
	Spanish: cumbre		Romanian: spic
			Occitan: espiga
			Catalan: espiga
			Spanish: espiga
			Portuguese: espiga
			Vegliote: spaica
			Italian: spiga
			Sardinian (Nuorese): ispica
cuncti	"all"	**omnes**	
			Old Italian: onni
da	"give"	**dona**	
	Gascon: da		French: donne
	Aragonese: da		Occitan: dona
	Spanish: da		Catalan: dona
	Portuguese: dá		Aragonese: dona
	Romansh: dai		
	Vegliote: du		
	Italian: dà		
	Sardinian: da		
	Romanian: dă		
denudare	"lay bare"	**discooperire**	
	French: dénuer 'deprive"		French: découvrir
	Spanish: desnudar		Occitan: descobrir
	Portuguese: desnudar 'undress"		Catalan: descobrir
			Spanish: descubrir
			Portuguese: descobrir
			Piedmontese: descörve
			Italian: discoprire
			Romanian: descoperire
detestare	"revile"	**blasphemare**	
			French: blâmer
			Occitan: blaimar

A Brief History of Latin and Romance Languages   *Reichenau Glosses, 8th Century*

4th Century Word

8th Century Replacement

        Catalan: blasmar
        Spanish: lastimar
        Portuguese: lastimar
        Vegliote: blasmur
        Old Italian: biastemmiare
        Sardinian (Nuorese): brastimar
        Romanian: blestemare

dilecta   "love"   **amata**

        Old French: amede
        French: aimée
        Occitan: aimada
        Catalan: amada
        Aragonese: amata
        Spanish: amada
        Portuguese: amada
        Venetian: amà
        Italian: amata
        Sardinian (Nuorese): amada

ducta   "lead"   **menata**
        Old French: duite   *Old French: menede*
        Old Occitan: ducha   *French: menée*
        Catalan: duita   *Occitan: menada*
        Old Spanish: ducha   *Catalan: menada*
        Old Italian: dotta   *Aragonese: menata*
        Romanian: dusă   *Italian: menata*
                Romanian: mânată

emit   "buy"   **comparauit**

        Old French: comprat
        Gascon: crompá
        Catalan: comprà
        Spanish: compró
        Portuguese: comprou
        Italian: comprò
        Romanian: cumpără 'bought'

ensis   "sword"   **gladius**

        Old French: glais 'sword-lily'
        French: glai 'sword-lily'
        Old Occitan: glazi
        Italian: ghiado 'sword'

escas   "food"   **cibos**
        French: esches
        Occitan: escas   *Spanish: cebos*
        Catalan: esques   *Portuguese: cevos 'bait'*
        Spanish: yescas
        Portuguese: escas 'bait"

A Brief History of Latin and Romance Languages   Reichenau Glosses, 8th Century

4th Century Word   8th Century Replacement

	Italian: esche 'bait, tinder"		
	Romanian: ieşti 'tinder"		
exacerbauerunt	"irritate"	**exasperauerunt**	
			Old French: asprirent
			Old Italian: asprirono
exaurire	"drain"	**scauare**	
			Old French: eschaver
			Occitan: escavar
			Spanish: escavar
			Portuguese: escavar
			Romansh: stgavar
			Italian: scavare
exterminabit	"uproot"	**eradicabit**	
			French: arracher
			Gascon: arrigar
			Old Occitan: arazigar
			Galician: arrigar
			Romanian: ridicare
exuerunt	"strip away"	**expoliauerunt**	
			Old French: espoillierent
			Italian: spogliarono
			Old Spanish: espojaron
			Galician: esbollaron
faretra	"arrow-case"	**teca sagittarum**	
			French: taie 'pillowcase'
			Italian: tega 'pod'
			Romanian: teacă 'case, sheath'
			Old French: saietes
			Occitan: sagetas
			Catalan: sagetes
			Spanish: saetas
			Portuguese: setas
			Old Italian: saette
			Sardinian (Nuorese): saittas
			Romanian: săgeţi
		cupra	
			Old French: cuivre
fatigatus	"tired"	**lassus**	
			French: las
			Occitan: las
femur	"thigh"	**coxa**	"hip"
			French: cuisse
			Occitan: cuèissa
			Catalan: cuixa

4th Century Word

8th Century Replacement

		cingolo	Spanish: *cuja* Portuguese: *cuxa* Piedmontese: *cheussa* Romansh: *cossa* Vegliote: *copsa* Italian: *coscia* Sardinian (Nuorese): *cossa* Romanian: *coapsă*
			Old French: *cengle* French: *sangle* Occitan: *cengla* Catalan: *cengle* Portuguese: *cilha* Venetian: *senghia* Italian: *cinghia* Neapolitan: *chienga* Romanian: *chingă*
ferus	"savage" Old French: *fiers 'proud"* French: *fier "proud"* Catalan: *fer "ugly"* Italian: *fiero 'proud"* Spanish: *fiero 'wild"*	**durus**	"harsh, severe" Old French: *durs* Romansh: *dirs* French: *dur* Occitan: *dur* Catalan: *dur* Spanish: *duro* Portuguese: *duro* Lombard (Milanese): *dur* Romansh: *dir* Vegliote: *doir* Italian: *duro*
feruet	"boil" Spanish: *hierve* Portuguese: *ferve* Romanian: *fierbe 'id."* Italian: *ferve 'has a fever"*	**bullit**	Old French: *bolt* French: *bout* Occitan: *bolhe* Catalan: *bulle* Spanish: *bulle 'id.'* Portuguese: *bule 'fidgets'* Italian: *bole* Neapolitan: *vodde* Sardinian (Nuorese): *buddit 'id.'*
fex	"dregs"	**lias**	French: *lies*
flare	"blow"	**suflare**	French: *souffler* Occitan: *soflar*

A Brief History of Latin and Romance Languages   Reichenau Glosses, 8th Century

4th Century Word   8th Century Replacement

			Aragonese: soflar
			Old Spanish: sollar
			Portuguese: soprar
			Romansh: suflar
			Italian: soffiare
			Romanian: suflare
flasconem	"flask"	**buticulam**	
	Old French: flascon		French: bouteille
	French: flacon		Occitan: botelha
	Occitan: flascon		
	Catalan: flascó		
	Spanish: frasco		
	Portuguese: frasco		
	Italian: fiasco		
fletur	"weep"	**planctur**	"there is mourning"
			French: plaindre
			Occitan: planher
			Catalan: plànyer
			Old Spanish: llanner
			Old Portuguese: changer
			Venetian: piànzar
			Vegliote: plungro
			Italian: piangere
			Neapolitan: chiagne
			Sicilian: chiànciri
			Sardinian (Nuorese): prangere
			Romanian: plângere
forum	"marketplace"	**mercatum**	
	Old French: fuer		Old French: marchiet
	French: fur 'extent"		French: marché
	Spanish: fuero 'law"		Occitan: mercat
	Romanian: for 'plaza"		Catalan: mercat
			Spanish: mercado
			Portuguese: mercado
			Romansh: marchà
			Venetian: marcà
			Italian: mercato
			Sardinian (Nuorese): mercadu
framea	"type of sword"	**gladius bisacutus**	
			French: besaiguë 'carpenter's tool'
			Italian: bisacuta 'double-edged'
furent	"steal"	**involent**	"sweep down, carry off"
	Italian: furino		Old French: emblent

A Brief History of Latin and Romance Languages *Reichenau Glosses, 8th Century*

4th Century Word

8th Century Replacement

	Romanian: fure		*Old Occitan: emblen*
			Old Catalan: emblen
			Italian: involino
furuus	"brown"	**brunus**	
			French: brun
			Occitan: brun
			Catalan: bru
			Spanish: bruno
			Portuguese: bruno
			Romansh: brun
			Vegliote: broin
			Italian: bruno
fusiles	"melt"	**fundutas**	
			French: fondues
			Occitan: fondudas
			Old Italian: fondute 'melted'
galea	"helmet"	**helmus**	
			Old French: helmeacc
			French: heaume
			Spanish: yelmo
			Portuguese: elmo
			Italian: elmo
genuit	"give birth"	**generauit**	
			Old French: gendrat
			French: engendra
			Gascon: engendrá
			Catalan: engendrà
			Spanish: engendró
			Portuguese: gerou
gratia	"thanks"	**merces**	"goods, wages"
			Old French: mercit
			French: merci
			Occitan: mercé 'mercy, thanks'
			Spanish: merced
			Portuguese: mercê 'mercy'
			Old Italian: mercé 'thanks'
			Italian: mercede 'mercy'
abenas	"reins"	**retinacula iumentorum**	
			Old French: rednes~resnes
			French: rênes
			Occitan: retnas
			Catalan: regnes
			Spanish: riendas
			Portuguese: rédeas

A Brief History of Latin and Romance Languages   Reichenau Glosses, 8th Century

4th Century Word   8th Century Replacement

			Italian: redine
			French: jument 'mare'
			Old Spanish: iumiento
			Spanish: jumento
			Portuguese: jumento
			Italian: giumento
			Neapolitan: jummèntafem 'pack animal'
arundine	"reed"	**ros**	
			Old French: ros
			Occitan: raus
			Old French: roseldim
			French: roseau
ebitatum	"weaken"	**bulcatum**	
			Old French: bolgiet
			French: bougé
			Occitan: bolegat
			Catalan: bellugat
			Aragonese: esbolligato 'stirred, agitated'
			Italian: bulicato 'boiled'
iacinctinas	"hyacinth"	**persas**	
	French: jacinthe		French: perse 'blue-green'
	Occitan: jacint		
	Catalan: jacint		
hiems	"winter"	**ibernus**	
			Old French: ivers
			Old Occitan: iverns
			Old French: ivern
			French: iver
			Occitan: ivèrn
			Catalan: hivern
			Spanish: invierno
			Asturian: iviernu
			Portuguese: invernu
			Romansh: inviern
			Vegliote: inviarno
			Italian: inverno
			Sardinian (Nuorese): iberru
			Romanian: iarnăfem
horreis	"granaries"	**spicariis**	
	Catalan: orri		Old Walloon: spir 'room for provisions'
	Asturian: orru		German: Speicher 'granary'
	Sardinian: orriu		
iacere	"throw"	**iactare**	

A Brief History of Latin and Romance Languages   Reichenau Glosses, 8*th* Century

4th Century Word		*8th Century Replacement*	
			French: jeter
			Occitan: getar
			Catalan: gitar
			Aragonese: chitar
			Spanish: echar
			Italian: gettare
			Neapolitan: jettà
			Sardinian (Nuorese): ghettare
ictus	"strike"	**colpus**	
	Portuguese: eito 'row"		Old French: cols
			Old French: colp
			French: coup
			Occitan: còp
			Catalan: cop
			Italian: colpo
id	"it"	**hoc**	"this"
			Old French: uec
			Occitan: o
			Catalan: ho 'this'
			Occitan: òc
			Old Catalan: oc 'yes'
iecore	"liver"	**ficato**	
	Portuguese: iguaria 'delicacies"		French: foie
			Asturian: fegadu
			Italian: fegato
			Friulian: fiât
			Romanian: ficat
			Spanish: higado
			Portuguese: figato
			Romansh: fio
			Neapolitan: ficato
			Sardinian (Nuorese): ficadu
			Occitan: fetge
			Catalan: fetge
			Piedmontese: fidic
			Lombard (Milanese): fideg
indutus	"dress"	**uestitus**	
			Old French: vestit
			Occitan: vestit
			Catalan: vestit
			Aragonese: vestito
			Spanish: vestido
			Portuguese: vestido
			Vegliote: vestiat

A Brief History of Latin and Romance Languages   Reichenau Glosses, 8th Century

4th Century Word   8th Century Replacement

			Italian: vestito
			Sardinian (Nuorese): bestiu
			Old French: vestut
			French: vêtu
			Old Italian: vestuto
institis	"bandages"	**fasciolis**	
			Old Italian: fasciuole
			Romanian: fâșioare
		nasculis	
			Old French: nasles
			Walloon: nâles
			Italian: nastrimasc
insultaret	"offend"	**inganaret**	
			Old French: enjaner
			Occitan: enganar
			Catalan: enganyar
			Spanish: engañar
			Italian: ingannare
			Romanian: îngânare
isset	"go"	**ambulasset**	"walk"
	Aragonese: isse		Old French: alast
	Ladin: jissa		French: alât
	Old Italian: gisse		Spanish: amblase
	Neapolitan: jesse		Italian: ambiasse
	Romanian: ise		Romanian: umblase
ita	"yes"	**sic**	
			French: si
			Occitan: si 'actually, yes'
			Catalan: sí
			Spanish: sí
			Portuguese: sim
			Romansh: schi
			Italian: sì 'yes'
			Romanian: și 'and'
iuger	"acre"	**iornalis**	
			Old French: jornal 'journal, measure of land'
			French: journal
			Occitan: jornal
			Italian: giornale 'journal'
iugulate	"kill"	**occidite**	
	Romanian: junghiați		Old French: ocidre
			Occitan: aucir
			Italian: uccidere
			Romanian: ucidere

A Brief History of Latin and Romance Languages *Reichenau Glosses, 8th Century*

4th Century Word

8th Century Replacement

ius	"law"	**legem**	Sardinian (Nuorese): occhidere
	Old Spanish: jur		Old French: lei
	Portuguese: jur		French: loi
	Italian: giure		Occitan: lei
			Catalan: llei
			Spanish: ley
			Portuguese: lei
			Piedmontese: lege
			Vegliote: lig
			Italian: legge
			Old Sardinian: leghe
			Romanian: lege
		potestatem	"power, authority"
			Old French: podestet
			Old Occitan: pozestat
			Old Italian: podestade
			Italian: podestà
labium	"tub"	**conca**	
			French: conche
			Occitan: conca
			Catalan: conca
			Spanish: cuenca
			Italian: conca 'basin, watershed'
			Sardinian (Nuorese): conca 'head'
lamento	"wail"	**ploro**	"weep"
			Old French: plour
			French: pleure
			Occitan: plori
			Catalan: ploro
			Ribagorçan: plloro
			Aragonese: ploro
			Spanish: lloro
			Portuguese: choro
			Piedmontese: piur
			Old Italian: pioro
laterum	"bricks"	**teularum**	"roof-tiles"
			Old French: tiules~teilles
			French: tuiles
			Occitan: teulas
			Catalan: teules
			Spanish: tejas
			Asturian: teya
			Portuguese: telhas

A Brief History of Latin and Romance Languages   Reichenau Glosses, 8ᵗʰ Century

4ᵗʰ Century Word   8ᵗʰ Century Replacement

			Vegliote: tacle
			Italian: tegole
			Sardinian (Nuorese): téulas 'tiles'
			Tuscan: tegghie
			Italian: teglie 'baking-trays'
lebes	"boiler"	**chaldaria**	
			Old French: chaldiere
			French: chaudière
			Gascon: caudera
			Catalan: caldera
			Spanish: caldera
			Portuguese: caldeira
			Vegliote: caldira
			Italian: caldaia
			Romanian: căldare
leua	"left"	**sinistra**	
			French: senestre
			Occitan: senèstra
			Old Spanish: siniestra
			Old Portuguese: sẽestra
			Romansh: saniestra
			Old Italian: sinestra
liberos	"children"	**infantes**	"babies"
			French: enfants
			Occitan: enfants
			Catalan: infants 'id.'
			Old Spanish: ifantes
			Old Portuguese: ifantes 'heirs-apparent'
			Romansh: uffants 'id.'
			Italian: fanti 'infantry'
litus	"shore"	**ripa**	
	Italian: lido		French: rive
			Occitan: riba
			Catalan: riba
			Spanish: riba
			Portuguese: riba
			Romansh: riva
			Vegliote: raipa
			Italian: riva
			Romanian: râpă
ludebant	"play"	**iocabant**	
			Old French: joevent
			French: jouaient

A Brief History of Latin and Romance Languages Reichenau Glosses, 8th Century

4th Century Word

8th Century Replacement

	Occitan: jogavan
	Catalan: jugaven
	Aragonese: chugaban
	Spanish: jugaban
	Portuguese: jogavam
	Romansh: giogavan
	Vegliote: jocua
	Italian: giocavano
	Romanian: jucau

luto "mud" **fecis** "dregs, sediment"
Italian: loto Italian: feci
Spanish: lodo Spanish: heces
Portuguese: lodo Portuguese: fezes
Romanian: lut
Sardinian: lutu

mala punica "pomegranates" **mala granata**

Occitan: milgrana
Catalan: magrana
Aragonese: mengrana
Old Spanish: milgrana
Spanish: granada
Portuguese: granada
Italian: melagrana

malus "mast" **mastus**

French: mât
Occitan: mast

manipulos "bundles" **garbas**
Old French: manoil French: gerbes
Old Italian: manocchi Occitan: garbas
Romanian: mănuchi Catalan: garbes
Old French: manoilz Aragonese: garbas
Catalan: manolls Ligurian: garbe
Spanish: manojos
Portuguese: molhos

mares "male animals" **masculi**

Old French: masle
Venetian: mas-ci
Friulian: mascli
Italian: maschi
Romanian: mascuri 'male pigs'
Old French: masles
French: mâles
Occitan: mascles
Catalan: mascles
Ribagorçan: mascllos

50

A Brief History of Latin and Romance Languages   Reichenau Glosses, 8th Century

4th Century Word   8th Century Replacement

			Aragonese: masclos
			Spanish: machos
			Portuguese: machos
			Romansh: mascels
			Sardinian (Nuorese): mascros
mergulum	"diver bird"	**coruum marinum**	
			French: cormoran
			Occitan: corb marin
			Catalan: corb marí
			Spanish: cuervo marino
			Portuguese: corvo marinho
milites	"soldiers"	**seruientes**	"servants"
			French: sergeants 'sergeants'
			Occitan: sirvents
			Catalan: servents
			Spanish: sirvientes 'servants'
minas	"threats"	**manaces**	
			French: menaces
			Gascon: miaças
			Occitan: menaças
			Old Spanish: menaças
			Old Portuguese: mẽaças
			Italian: minacce
mutuo acceperam	"borrow"	**impruntatum habeo**	
			Old French: ai empruntet
			Occitan: ai empruntat
			Romanian: am imprumutat
mutuum dare	"lend"	**prestare**	"provide, furnish"
			French: prêter
			Occitan: prestar
			Catalan: prestar
			Spanish: prestar
			Portuguese: prestar
			Italian: prestare
necetur	"kill"	**occidetur**	
	Old French: neier		Old French: ocidre
	French: noyer		Occitan: aucir
	Occitan: negar		Italian: uccidere
	Spanish: anegar+pref		Romanian: ucidere
	Italian: annegare+pref		Sardinian (Nuorese): occhidere
	Aromanian: necare		
nemini	"nobody"	**nulli**	
	Romanian: nimeni		French: nul

A Brief History of Latin and Romance Languages *Reichenau Glosses, 8th Century*

4th Century Word

8th Century Replacement

			Occitan: nul
			Catalan: nul
			Vegliote: nul
			Italian: nullo
			Sardinian (Nuorese): nuddu
			Sicilian: nuḍḍu 'none, futile'
nent	"weave"	**filant**	
			French: filent
			Gascon: hilan
			Occitan: filan
			Catalan: filen
			Italian: filano
			Spanish: hilan
			Portuguese: filam
nonnulli	"several"	**multi**	
			Old French: molt
			Old Occitan: much
			Italian: molti
			Romanian: mulți
			Old French: molz
			Catalan: mols
			Spanish: muchos
			Asturian: munchos
			Portuguese: muitos
non pepercit	"not spare"	**non sparniauit**	
			Old French: nen esparnat
			Italian: non sparagnò
nouacula	"razor"	**rasorium**	
	Catalan: navalla		*French: rasoir*
	Spanish: navaja		*Occitan: rasor*
	Asturian: navaja		*Catalan: raor*
	Portuguese: navalha		*Spanish: rasero*
			Italian: rasoio
nouerca	"stepmother"	**matrastra**	
	Aromanian: nuearcã		*French: marâtre*
			Occitan: mairastra
			Catalan: madrastra
			Spanish: madrastra
			Portuguese: madrasta
			Piedmontese: marastra
			Lombard (Milanese): madrastra
nosse	"know"	**scire**	
			Romanian: știre
			Sardinian (Nuorese): ischire
nutare	"wobble"	**cancellare**	"criss-cross"

A Brief History of Latin and Romance Languages   Reichenau Glosses, 8th Century

4th Century Word   8th Century Replacement

			French: chanceler
ocreas	"greaves"	**husas**	
			Old French: hueses
			Old Spanish: uesas
			Old Portuguese: osas
			Old Italian: uose
offendas	"drive away"	**abattas**	
			French: abattes
			Occitan: abatas
			Catalan: abatis
			Spanish: abatas
			Portuguese: abatas
			Italian: abbatta
onager	"wild donkey"	**asinus saluaticus**	"asinus" = donkey
			Old French: asnes
			Old French: asne
			French: âne
			Gascon: aso
			Occitan: asne
			Catalan: ase
			Spanish: asno
			Portuguese: asno
			Ligurian: âze
			Piedmontese: aso
			Lombard (Milanese): asen
			Romansh: asen
			Venetian: axeno
			Italian: asino
			Romanian: asen
			Sardinian (Nuorese): áinu
onustus	"burden"	**carcatus**	
			Old French: chargiez
			Old Occitan: cargats
			Old French: chargiet
			French: chargé
			Occitan: cargat
			Catalan: carregat
			Spanish: cargado
			Portuguese: carregado
			Italian: caricato
			Romanian: încărcat
oppidis	"towns"	**ciuitatibus**	
			French: cités
			Occitan: ciutats

A Brief History of Latin and Romance Languages   Reichenau Glosses, 8th Century

4th Century Word   8th Century Replacement

		castellis	Catalan: ciutats Spanish: ciudades Portuguese: cidades Romansh: citads Venetian: sità Old Italian: cittadi Italian: città 'cities' Romanian: cetăți 'fortresses' "fortresses" Old French: chastel Old Occitan: castel Venetian: castełi Old Italian: castegli Italian: castelli Sicilian: casteḍḍi Old French: chastels French: châteaux Gascon: castèths Occitan: castèls Catalan: castells Spanish: castillos Asturian: castiellos Portuguese: castelos Romansh: chastès Sardinian (Nuorese): casteddos
opilio	"shepherd"	**berbicarius**	Old French: bergiers Old French: bergier French: berger Limousin: bargier Romanian: berbecar Sardinian (Nuorese): berbecarju
oportet	"be fitting"	**conuenit**	French: convient Occitan: conven Catalan: convé Spanish: conviene Portuguese: convém Italian: conviene Romanian: cuvine
optimos	"best"	**meliores**	"better" French: meilleurs Occitan: melhors Catalan: millors Spanish: mejores

A Brief History of Latin and Romance Languages   Reichenau Glosses, 8th Century

4th Century Word   8th Century Replacement

			Asturian: meyores
			Portuguese: melhores
			Romansh: megliers
			Italian: migliori
optimum	"best"	**ualde bonum**	
			Old French: buen, bon
			French: bon
			Occitan: bon
			Catalan: bo
			Spanish: bueno
			Portuguese: bom
			Romansh: bun
			Vegliote: bun
			Italian: buono
			Romanian: bun
ore	"mouth"	**bucca**	"cheek"
			French: bouche
			Occitan: boca
			Catalan: boca
			Spanish: boca
			Portuguese: boca
			Romansh: boca
			Vegliote: buca
			Italian: bocca 'mouth'
			Romanian: bucă 'cheek'
ostendit	"show"	**monstrauit**	
			Old French: mostrat
			French: montra
			Gascon: mostrà
			Catalan: mostrà
			Spanish: mostró
			Portuguese: mostrou
			Italian: mostrò
			Romanian: mustră
oues	"sheep"	**berbices**	
	Romanian: oi		French: brebis
	French: ouailles		Old Occitan: berbitz
	Occitan: oelhas		Old Italian: berbici
	Limousin: auvelhas		
	Catalan: ovelles		Sardinian (Nuorese): berbeches
	Aragonese: uellas		Romanian: berbeci
	Spanish: ovejas		
	Portuguese: ovelhas		
paliurus	"Christs thorn"	**cardonis**	
			French: chardon

A Brief History of Latin and Romance Languages   Reichenau Glosses, 8th Century

4th Century Word

8th Century Replacement

Occitan: cardon
Italian: cardone
Sicilian: carduni
Spanish: cardo
Portuguese: cardo
Italian: cardo
Sicilian: cardo

pallium "cloak"   **drappum**

French: drap
Occitan: drap
Catalan: drap
Spanish: trapo
Portuguese: trapo
Vegliote: drap
Italian: drappo
Sardinian (Nuorese): drappu

papilionis "tent"   **trauis**
Old French: paveilun   Old French: tresnom
'butterfly, pavilion"
French: pavillon   Old French: tref 'tent, beam'
Occitan: pabalhon   Old Occitan: trau
Catalan: pavelló   Portuguese: trave
Spanish: pabellón   Italian: trave
Italian: padiglione 'pavilion"
French: papillon
Occitan: parpalhon
Catalan: papallona
Old Italian: parpaglione
'butterfly"

pabula "blister"   **uisica**

French: vessie
Occitan: vessiga
Catalan: veixiga
Spanish: vejiga
Asturian: vexiga
Portuguese: bexiga
Italian: vescica
Sardinian (Nuorese): bussica
Romanian: băşică 'blister, bladder'

paria "alike"   **similia**
French: paire   Old French: sembles
Piedmontese: paira   Old Occitan: sembles
Italian: paia 'pair(s)"

pera "bag"   **sportellam** "little basket"
    Old Occitan: esportèla

A Brief History of Latin and Romance Languages   Reichenau Glosses, 8th Century

4th Century Word   8th Century Replacement

			Spanish: esportilla
			Old Italian: sportella
			Sardinian (Nuorese): isportedda
peribet	"bear"	**perportat**	
			French: il porte témoignage
			Italian: porta testimonianza
pes	"foot"	**pedis**	
			Old French: pieznom
			Old Occitan: pes
			Old French: piet
			French: pied
			Occitan: pè
			Catalan: peu
			Aragonese: piet
			Spanish: pié
			Portuguese: pe
			Romansh: pe
			Vegliote: pi
			Italian: piede
			Sardinian (Nuorese): pede
			Old Romanian: piez
pignus	"pledge"	**uuadius**	
	Old Spanish: pennos		French: gage
	Spanish: peño		Occitan: gatge 'will, testament'
	Romansh: pegn		
	Italian: pegno		
	Spanish: prenda		
	Old Italian: pegnora		
	Portuguese: penhor		
pingues	"fat"	**grassi**	
			Old French: gras
			Vegliote: gres
			Italian: grassi
			Romanian: grași
			French: gras
			Catalan: grassos
			Spanish: grasos
			Portuguese: grassos
			Romansh: gras
			Sardinian (Nuorese): grassos
plaustra	"carts"	**carra**	
			Romansh: care
			Old French: char
			Italian: carri
			French: chars

4th Century Word | | 8th Century Replacement

4th Century Word		8th Century Replacement	
			Occitan: carris
			Catalan: carros
			Spanish: carros
			Portuguese: carros
pulempta	"barley"	**farina**	"flour"
	Vegliote: polianta		French: farine
	Italian: polenta		Gascon: haria
	Sardinian: pulenta		Occitan: farina
			Catalan: farina
			Spanish: harina
			Portuguese: farinha
			Piedmontese: farin-a
			Romansh: farina
			Vegliote: faraina
			Italian: farina
			Sardinian (Nuorese): farina
			Romanian: făină
pupillam	"pupil"	**nigrum in oculo**	
			French: le noir de l'œil
ponatur	"put"	**mittatur**	
	French: pondre		French: mettre
	Gascon: póner		Gascon: méter
	Occitan: pondre		Occitan: metre
	Catalan: pondre		Catalan: metre
	Ribagorçan: ponre 'lay an egg"		Ribagorçan: metre
	Spanish: poner		Spanish: meter
	Portuguese: põer		Portuguese: meter
	Portuguese: pôr		Italian: mettere
	Italian: porre		Sardinian (Nuorese): mintere
	Sardinian: ponnere		
	Romanian: punere 'put, place"		
ponderatus	"burdened"	**grauiatus**	
			Old French: gregiez
poplite	"hock"	**iuncture ianiculorum**	
			French: jointures
			Occitan: jonchuras
			Catalan: juntures
			Spanish: junturas
			Portuguese: junturas
			Italian: giunture
			Old French: genoil
			Vegliote: zenacle
			Italian: ginocchi

A Brief History of Latin and Romance Languages   Reichenau Glosses, 8th Century

4th Century Word   8th Century Replacement

			Romanian: genunchi
			Old French: genoilz
			French: genoux
			Occitan: genolhs
			Catalan: genolls
			Aragonese: chenollos
			Spanish: hinojos
			Portuguese: joelhos
			Romansh: schanugls
			Sardinian (Nuorese): brenucos

pruina "frost"   **gelata**
French: bruine 'drizzle"   Old French: gelede
Old Occitan: bruina "frost"   French: gelée
Venetian: puìna 'ricotta cheese"   Occitan: gelada
Italian: brina 'frost"
     Catalan: gelada
     Spanish: helada
     Portuguese: geada
     Piedmontese: gelada
     Italian: gelata
     Sardinian (Nuorese): ghelada

pugione "dagger"   **lancea** "spear"
     French: lance
     Occitan: lança
     Catalan: llança
     Spanish: lanza
     Portuguese: lança
     Italian: lancia
     Sardinian (Nuorese): lantza

pulchra "beautiful"   **bella**
     French: belle
     Occitan: bèla
     Catalan: bella
     Aragonese: bella
     Romansh: bella
     Vegliote: biala
     Italian: bella
     Sicilian: bedda

pusillum "small"   **paruum**
     Old French: parf 'small'
     Portuguese: parvo 'small, dumb'
     Old Italian: parvolo
     Italian: pargolo 'boy'

pustula "blister"   **malis clauis**
     French: clou 'nail, pustule'

A Brief History of Latin and Romance Languages   *Reichenau Glosses, 8th Century*

4th Century Word   8th Century Replacement

			Old Occitan: clau
			Catalan: clau
			Ribagorçan: cllau
			Aragonese: clau
			Spanish: clavo
			Portuguese: cravu
			Piedmontese: ciòv
			Old Italian: chiavo
			Sardinian (Nuorese): cravu 'nail'

regit   "rule"   **gubernat**
Italian: regge   *Old French: governet*
Sardinian: reghet   *French: gouverne*
     Occitan: governa
     Catalan: governa
     Spanish: gobierna
     Portuguese: governa
     Italian: governa
     Sardinian (Nuorese): cuberrat

remetieur   "remeasure"   **remensurabit**
Spanish: medir   *French: mesurer*
Portuguese: medir   *Occitan: mesurar*
Sardinian: metire   *Catalan: mesurar*
     Spanish: mesurar
     Portuguese: mesurar
     Romansh: mesirar
     Italian: misurare
     Romanian: măsurare

repente   "suddenly"   **subito**
     Old French: sode
     Occitan: sopte
     Catalan: sopte

reppererunt   "find"   **inuenerunt**
     Old French: *envindrent
     Old Sardinian: *imbennerun

res   "thing"   **causa**   "subject matter"
Gascon: arrés   *French: chose*
Occitan: res   *Occitan: causa*
Catalan: res 'nothing"   *Catalan: cosa*
Spanish: res   *Spanish: cosa*
Sardinian: rese 'head of cattle"   *Old Portuguese: cousa*
Old French: rien 'thing"   *Portuguese: coisa*
French: rien   *Romansh: chossa*
Limousin: ren   *Vegliote: causa*
Gascon: arrén   *Italian: cosa*

A Brief History of Latin and Romance Languages   Reichenau Glosses, 8th Century

4th Century Word   8th Century Replacement

	Portuguese: ren		Old Sardinian: casa
	Galician: ren 'nothing"		
respectant	"look back"	**reuuardant**	
	Portuguese: respeitam		French: regardent
	Italian: rispettano 'respect"		Occitan: gardan-pref
			Catalan: guarden-pref
			Spanish: guardan-pref
			Portuguese: guardam-pref
			Lombard (Milanese): vàrden
			Romansh: vurdan-pref
			Italian: riguardano
			Neapolitan: guardano-pref
restant	"stay"	**remanent**	
			Old French: remainent
			Catalan: romanen
			Italian: rimangano
			Old Spanish: remane
			Romanian: rămân
reus	"guilty"	**culpabilis**	
	Vegliote: ri		French: coupable
	Italian: rio		Occitan: colpable
	Romanian: rău 'bad, evil"		Italian: colpevole 'guilty'
reueretur	"fear"	**uerecundatur**	"feel shame"
			Old French: vergondet
rostrum	"beak"	**beccus**	
	Spanish: rostro		Old French: bes
	Portuguese: rosto 'face"		French: bec
	Romanian: rost 'mouth"		Occitan: bèc
			Catalan: bec
			Spanish: pico
			Portuguese: bico
			Italian: becco
rufa	"reddish"	**sora**	
			French: saure 'smoked'
			Occitan: saura 'yellow'
			Catalan: saura 'dark yellow'
ruga	"wrinkle"	**fruncetura**	
	French: rue		French: fronçure
	Limousin: rua 'street"		
	Italian: ruga 'id."		
	Aromanian: arugã 'sheep-gate"		
rupem	"rock"	**petram**	
	Italian: rupe 'cliff"		Old French: piedre
			French: pierre

4th Century Word

		Occitan: pèira
		Catalan: pedra
		Spanish: piedra
		Portuguese: pedra
		Vegliote: pitra
		Italian: pietra
		Romanian: piatră
saga	"cloak"	**cortina**
	French: saie	*French: courtine*
	Old Spanish: saya	*Occitan: cortina*
	Portuguese: saia 'skirt"	*Catalan: cortina*
		Spanish: cortina
		Old Portuguese: cortinha
		Italian: cortina
sagma	"packsaddle"	**soma**
		French: somme 'packsaddle'
		Occitan: sauma 'female donkey'
		Catalan: salma 'ton'
		Italian: soma 'load, burden'
		Italian: salma 'corpse'
		sella
		French: selle
		Occitan: sèla
		Catalan: sella
		Old Spanish: siella
		Spanish: silla
		Portuguese: sela
		Vegliote: siala
		Italian: sella
		Sicilian: sedda
		Sardinian (Nuorese): sedda
		Romanian: șa 'saddle'
saniore	"healthy"	**plus sano**
		French: plus sain
		Occitan: pus san
		Old Catalan: pus san
		Old Portuguese: chus são
		Ligurian: chu san
		Piedmontese: pi san
		Italian: più sano
		Sardinian (Nuorese): prus sanu
sarcina	"package"	**bisatia**
	Romanian: sarcină	*French: besace*
	Aromanian: sartsinã	*Gascon: besaça*
		Occitan: biaço

A Brief History of Latin and Romance Languages — Reichenau Glosses, 8th Century — 8th Century Replacement

A Brief History of Latin and Romance Languages   Reichenau Glosses, 8th Century

4th Century Word   8th Century Replacement

sartago	"pan"	**patella**	Italian: bisaccia
	Occitan: sartan		Old French: padela
	Neapolitan: sartayine		French: poêle
	Spanish: sartén		Occitan: padèla
	Galician: sartaña		Catalan: paella
	Portuguese: sertã		Spanish: padilla
	Sardinian: sartaghine		Romansh: padella
			Italian: padella
			Sicilian: paredḍa
scinifes	"gnats"	**cincellas**	
			Old French: cinceles
			Venetian: sginsałe
			Italian: zanzare
			Romanian: țânțarimasc
segetes	"crops"	**messes**	
			Catalan: messes
			Italian: messi
			Spanish: mieses
			Portuguese: messes
			Old French: meissons
			French: moissons
			Occitan: meissons
semel	"once"	**una uice**	
			Old French: une feis
			French: une fois
			Occitan: una vets
			Spanish: una vez
			Portuguese: uma vez
sepulta	"interr"	**sepelita**	
	Vegliote: sepualta		Old French: sevelide
	Italian: sepoltalit		French: ensevelie
			Occitan: sebelida
			Catalan: sebollida
			Italian: seppellita
sindone	"cloth"	**linciolo**	
	Italian: sindone		French: linceul
			Occitan: lençòl
			Catalan: llençol
			Spanish: lenzuelo
			Portuguese: lençol
			Romansh: lenziel
			Vegliote: linžòl
			Italian: lenzuolo
singulariter	"individually"	**solamente**	

A Brief History of Latin and Romance Languages   *Reichenau Glosses, 8th Century*

4th Century Word   8th Century Replacement

			Old French: solement
			French: seulement
			Occitan: solament
			Catalan: solament
			Old Spanish: solamiente
			Portuguese: somente
			Italian: solamente

si uis   "if want"   **si uoles**

Old French: se vuels
French: *si veux
Occitan: se vòls
Catalan: si vols
Romansh: sche vuls
Vegliote: se vule
Italian: se vuoi
Sardinian (Nuorese): si boles

solutis   "free"   **disligatis**
Old French: soluz 'resolved, paid"

Old French: desliez

French: déliés
Old Spanish: deslegados
Old Portuguese: deslegados
Italian: sligati
Romanian: dezlegați

sortileus   "fortune-teller"   **sorcerus**

French: sorcier

spatula   "palm-frond"   **rama palmarum**
Old French: espalle
French: épaule
Occitan: espatla
Catalan: espattla
Spanish: espalda
Portuguese: espalda
Venetian: spała
Italian: spalla
Sicilian: spaḍḍa

Old French: raime
French: rame
Occitan: rama
Catalan: rama
Spanish: rama 'branch'
Old French: palmes
French: paumes
Occitan: palmas
Catalan: palmes
Spanish: palmas
Portuguese: palmas
Italian: palme
Sardinian (Nuorese): parmas
Romanian: palme

stercora   "excrement"   **femus**
Old Spanish: estierco
Portuguese: esterco
Italian: sterco

Old French: fiens
Occitan: fens
Catalan: fem

A Brief History of Latin and Romance Languages   Reichenau Glosses, 8th Century

4th Century Word   8th Century Replacement

4th C.	Meaning / Descendants	8th C.	Meaning / Descendants
submersi	Romanian: șterc Spanish: estiércol "drown" Italian: sommersi	**necati**	Aragonese: fiemo "murdered" Old French: ocidre Occitan: aucir Italian: uccidere Romanian: ucidere Sardinian (Nuorese): occhidere
subtilissima	"very" Old French: sotil Old Occitan: sotil Old Catalan: Sotil Italian: sottile Sardinian: suttile Romanian: subțire	**perpittita**	French: petite Catalan: petita Occitan: petita
succendunt	"ignite"	**sprendunt**	French: éprennent
sudario	"priests gown" Vegliote: sedarul 'handkerchief'	**fanonem**	French: fanon 'papal gown'
sulcis	"ridges" Italian: solchi Neapolitan: surchi Catalan: solcs Spanish: surcos Portuguese: sucos Sardinian: surcos	**rige**	Old French: reies French: raies Occitan: regas
sus	"pig" Sardinian: sue	**porcus**	Old French: pors salvadges French: porc sauvage Occitan: pòrc salvatge Catalan: porc salvatge Romansh: portg selvadi Vegliote: puarc salvutic Italian: porco salvatico Romanian: porc sălbatic
talpas	"moles" French: taupes Occitan: talpas Catalan: talps Spanish: topos Galician: toupas Italian: talpe Sardinian: tarpas	**muli**	French: mulotdim 'field mouse'
tectum	"roof"	**solarium**	"roof-terrace"

A Brief History of Latin and Romance Languages — Reichenau Glosses, 8th Century

4th Century Word   8th Century Replacement

Old French: teit   *French: solier*
French: toit   *Gascon: solèr 'loft'*
Gascon: teit
Occitan: tech
Spanish: techo
Galician: teito
Portuguese: teto
Piedmontese: tèit
Lombard (Milanese): tecc
Romansh: tetg
Vegliote: tiat
Italian: tetto

tedet "annoy"   **anoget**

French: ennuie
Occitan: enoja
Catalan: enutja
Spanish: enoja
Portuguese: enoja
Italian: uggia-pref

tedio "monotony"   **tepiditas**

Old French: tieve
French: tiède
Limousin: tedde
Occitan: tèbe
Catalan: tebi
Spanish: tibio
Portuguese: tíbio
Italian: tiepido
Sardinian (Nuorese): tépiu 'lukewarm'

tereo "thresh"   **tribulo**

Old French: trible, triule
Catalan: trillo
Spanish: trillo
Portuguese: trilho
Italian: tribbio
Sardinian (Nuorese): triulo

teristrum "garment"   **cufia**

Old French: cofie
French: coife
Gascon: còho
Occitan: còfa
Portuguese: coifa

         uitta "headband"

Old French: vete

4th Century Word — 8th Century Replacement

4th Century Word		8th Century Replacement	
			Catalan: veta
			Spanish: beta
			Portuguese: fita
			Italian: vetta
			Romanian: bată
torax	"cuirass"	**brunia**	
			Old French: bronie
			French: broigne
			Old Occitan: bronha
trabem	"beam"	**trastrum**	"crossbeam"
			Old French: traste 'crossbeam'
			Spanish: trasto
			Portuguese: traste 'junk'
transferent	"carry across"	**transportent**	
			Old French: tresportent
			Old Italian: traportano
transgredere	"pass by"	**ultra alare**	
			Old French: oltre aler
transmeare	"swim across"	**transnotare**	
			Old French: *tresnoder
			Old Italian: tranotare
			Old French: noder
			Romansh: nodar
			Vegliote: notur
			Old Italian: notare
			Romanian: înotare
tugurium	"hut"	**cauana**	
			Old French: chavane
			Occitan: cabana
			Catalan: cabanya
			Aragonese: capanna
			Spanish: cabaña
			Portuguese: cabana
			Italian: capanna
turibulum	"incense burner"	**incensarium**	
			Old French: encensier 'incense burner'
			French: encensier 'rosemary'
thurmas	"crowds"	**fulcos**	
	Italian: torme		Old French: fols
	Friulian: torme		French: foulesfem
	Romanian: turme		Old Occitan: folcs
	Sardinian: trumas		Gascon: hurasfem
			Occitan: fulasfem
			Galician: foulasfem

A Brief History of Latin and Romance Languages   *Reichenau Glosses, 8th Century*

4th Century Word   8th Century Replacement

tutamenta   "defenses"   **defendementa**

                                                          Old French: defendemenz

uecors   "senseless"   **esdarnatus**

                                                          French: dial, darne 'stumbling, impulsive'

ueru   "roasting-spit"   **spidus**
      Old French: veroil   *Old French: espeiznom*
      French: verrou   *Old French: espeitacc*
      Provençal: ferrolh   *French: époi*
      Occitan: varrolh   *Spanish: espeto*
      Catalan: forrolh   *Portuguese: espeto*
      Spanish: cerrojo
      Portuguese: ferrolho
      Italian: verrocchio

uespertiliones   "bats"   **calues sorices**

      Asturian: esperteyu   *French: chauves-souris*
      Old Italian: vipistrello
      Italian: pipistrello

uestis   "garment"   **rauba**
      French: vêtement   *French: robe*
      Romansh: büschmaint   *Occitan: rauba*
      Vegliote: vestemiant   *Catalan: roba*
      Romanian: veșmânt   *Spanish: ropa*
                                        Portuguese: roupa
                                        Italian: roba

uim   "power"   **fortiam**

                                        French: force
                                        Occitan: força
                                        Catalan: força
                                        Spanish: fuerza
                                        Portuguese: força
                                        Romansh: forza
                                        Italian: forza

uiscera   "guts"   **intralia**

                                        French: entrailles
                                        Occitan: entralhas
                                        Old French: entragnes
                                        Catalan: entranyes
                                        Spanish: entrañas
                                        Portuguese: entranhas

ungues   "fingernails"   **ungulas**

                                        French: ongles
                                        Occitan: onglas
                                        Catalan: ungles

A Brief History of Latin and Romance Languages   Reichenau Glosses, 8th Century

4th Century Word   8th Century Replacement

			Spanish: uñas
			Portuguese: unhas
			Romansh: unglas
			Vegliote: jongle
			Italian: unghie
			Romanian: unghii
			Sardinian (Nuorese): ungras
uorax	"devouring"	**manducans**	"chewing"
			French: mangeant
			Occitan: manjant
			Catalan: menjant
			Romansh: mangiond
			Old Italian: manicando
			Romanian: mâncând
			Sardinian (Nuorese): mandicande
urguet	"urge forward"	**adastat**	
			Old Occitan: adasta
usuris	"loan interest"	**lucris**	
			profits, wealth
			Aromanian: lucri 'objects'
			Old French: loirs 'revenues, assets'
			Spanish: logros
			Portuguese: logros 'achievements'
utere	"use"	**usitare**	
			French: use
			Occitan: usa
			Catalan: usa
			Spanish: usa
			Portuguese: usa
			Italian: usa
utres	"wineskins"	**folli**	
	Spanish: odres		Old French: fols
	Portuguese: odres		French: fous
	Italian: otri		Occitan: fòls
	Aromanian: utri		Catalan: folls 'madmen, fools'
			Spanish: fuelles
			Portuguese: foles
			Old Italian: folli
			Romanian: foale
			Sardinian (Nuorese): foddes 'bellows'
uuas	"grapes"	**racemos**	"clusters, bunches, grapes"
	Spanish: uvas		French: raisins

A Brief History of Latin and Romance Languages — Reichenau Glosses, 8th Century

4th Century Word *8th Century Replacement*

Portuguese: uvas
Romansh: ieuvas
Italian: uve
Vegliote: joive
Aromanian: aue

Occitan: rasim
Catalan: raïms 'grapes'
Spanish: racimos
Portuguese: racimos 'clusters'
Italian: racimoli 'clusters'

Veronese Riddle, 8th-9th Century

Old Italian

Se pareba boves
alba pratalia araba
albo versorio teneba
negro semen seminaba

English

He led oxen in front of him
He ploughed a white field
He held a white plough
He sowed a black seed

Word List

Old Italian	English	Latin
alba	white	album
albo	a-white	album
araba	he-plowed	arabat
boves	oxen	bovis
negro	black	nigrum
pareba	led	parere
pratalia	fields	agros
se	he	se
semen	seed	semen
seminaba	he-sowed	seminabat
teneba	he-held	tenebat
versorio	plough	versorium

Commodilla Catacomb, 8th-10th Century

Latin	Literal	English
Non dicere ille secrita ab boce.	Not to-speak the secrets out-of the-mouth.	Do not speak the secrets out of the mouth.

Word List

Vulgar Latin	English	Latin
ab	out-of	*ab*
boce	the-mouth	*bucca*
dicere	to-speak	*dicere*
ille	the	*those*
non	not	*non*
secrita	secrets	*secreta*

Oaths of Strasbourg, 9th Century

Old French	Literal	English
Pro Deo amur et pro christian poblo et nostro commun saluament,	For God the-love-of and for christian the-people and our common salvation,	For the love of God and for the christian people and our common salvation,
d'ist di in auant,	of-this day in-to future,	from this day forward,
in quant Deus sauir et podir me dunat,	in how-much God wisdom and power me gives,	as much as God gives me wisdom and strength,
si saluarai eo cist meon fradre Karlo,	so will-protect I to-this my brother Charles,	so I will protect my brother Charles,
et in adiudha et in cadhuna cosa si cum om per dreit son fradra saluar dist,	and in aid and in every thing so as a-man by right his brother to-protect should,	and aid him in everything as a man should to protect his brother,
in o quid il mi altresi fazet.	in in-so-far-as that he to-me likewise shall-do.	insofar as that he does likewise for me.
Et ab Ludher nul plaid nunquam prindrai qui meon uol cist meon fradre Karle in damno sit.	And with Lothair not council never shall-take which my will to-this my brother Charles in damnation may-be.	And with Lothair I shall take no council of my own will that may place Charles in danger.
- - -	- - -	- - -
Si Lodhuuigs sagrament, que son fradre Karlo iurat, conservat,	If Louis sacrament, which his brother Charles sworn, keeps,	If Louis keeps this sacrament, which he has sworn with his brother Charles,
et Karlus meos sendra de suo part lo fraint,	and Charles mine lord of his part it breaks,	and my lord Charles on his part breaks it,
si io returnar non l'int pois,	if I dissuade not him-from am-able,	if I cannot dissuade him,
ne io ne neuls, cui eo returnar int pois,	neither I nor no-one, who I dissuade him-from am-able,	neither I nor anyone could dissuade him from it,
in nulla aiudha contra Lodhuuig nun li ju er.	in no aid against Louis not to-him I will-be.	then I shall not give aid against Louis.

Word List

Old French	English	Latin
ab	with	ab
adiudha	aid	adiuto
aiudha	aid	adiuto
altresi	likewise	alter-si
amur	the-love-of	amor
auant	future	ab-ante
cadhuna	every	catunum
christian	christian	christianus
cist	to-this	ecce-iste

A Brief History of Latin and Romance Languages   Oaths of Strasbourg, 9th Century

Old French	English	Latin
commun	common	communitas
conservat	keeps	conservare
contra	against	contra
cosa	thing	causa
cui	who	qui
cum	as	cum
damno	damnation	damnatio
de	of	de
Deo	God (name)	Deo
Deus	God (name)	Deus
di	day	diem
dist	should	de-iste
d'ist	of-this	de-iste
dreit	right	directus
dunat	gives	donat
eo	I	ego
er	will-be	erit
et	and	et
fazet	shall-do	faciam
fradra	brother	frater
fradre	brother	frater
fraint	breaks	fracture
il	he	ille
in	in-to	in
in	in	in
int	him-from	inter
io	I	ego
iurat	sworn	iurat
ju	I	ego
Karle	Charles (name)	Carolus
Karlo	Charles (name)	Carolus
Karlus	Charles (name)	Carolus
li	to-him	ille
l'int	him-from	ille-inter
lo	it	lo
Lodhuuigs	Louis (name)	Ludovicus
Lodhuuuig	Louis (name)	Ludovicus
Ludher	Lothair (name)	Ludovicus
me	me	me
meon	my	meum
meos	mine	meus
mi	to-me	mihi
ne	neither	nec

A Brief History of Latin and Romance Languages   Oaths of Strasbourg, 9ᵗʰ Century

Old French	*English*	*Latin*
ne	nor	*nec*
neuls	no-one	*nullus*
non	not	*non*
nostro	our	*nostrum*
nul	not	*nullus*
nulla	no	*nullus*
nun	not	*non*
nunquam	never	*nunquam*
o	in-so-far-as	*in*
om	a-man	*hominus*
part	part	*pars*
per	by	*per*
plaid	council	*placitum*
poblo	the-people	*populum*
podir	power	*potentem*
pois	am-able	*possum*
prindrai	shall-take	*prendere*
Pro	for	*pro*
quant	how-much	*quanto*
que	which	*que*
qui	which	*que*
quid	that	*quid*
returnar	dissuade	*re-torno*
sagrament	sacrament	*sacramentum*
saluament	salvation	*salvationem*
saluar	to-protect	*salvamentum*
saluarai	will-protect	*salvare*
sauir	wisdom	*sapere*
sendra	lord	*seniorem*
si	so	*si*
si	if	*si*
sit	may-be	*sit*
son	his	*suus*
suo	his	*suus*
uol	will	*voluntatem*

Canticle of Saint Eulalia, 9th Century

Old French	Literal	English
Buona pulcella fut eulalia.	Good girl was Eulalia.	Eulalia was a good girl,
Bel auret corps bellezour anima.	Graceful had body beautiful soul.	She had a beautiful body, a soul more beautiful still.
Voldrent la veintre li deo Inimi.	Wanted the kill the God Enemies.	The enemies of God wanted to overcome her,
Voldrent la faire diaule seruir.	Wanted her do the-devil serve.	they wanted to make her serve the devil.
Elle no'nt eskoltet les mals conselliers.	She did-not-want listen the evil counsellers.	She does not listen to the evil counsellors,
Qu'elle deo raneiet chi maent sus en ciel.	which-she God deny who resides up in heaven.	to deny God, who lives up in heaven.
Ne por or ned argent ne paramenz.	Not for gold neither silver nor adornments.	Not for gold, nor silver, nor jewels,
Por manatce regiel ne preiement.	For threats regal nor prayers.	not for the king's threats or entreaties,
Niule cose non la pouret omque pleier.	Nothing thing not she able once bend.	nothing could ever persuade the girl
La polle sempre non amast lo deo menestier.	She girl always not to-love the God service.	not to love continually the service of God.
E por o fut presentede maximiien.	And for this was presented Maximian.	And for this reason she was brought before Maximian,
Chi rex eret a cels dis soure pagiens.	Who king was in those days over the-pagans.	who was king in those days over the pagans.
Il li enortet dont lei nonque chielt.	He her encourages but-then she never was-bothered.	He exhorts her — but she does not care —
Qued elle fuiet lo nom christiien.	That she flee the name Christian.	to abandon the Christian name;
Ell'ent adunet lo suon element.	she-then worships the his god.	And subsequently worship his god.
Melz sostendreiet les empedementz,	Better she-would-undergo the persecution,	She would rather undergo persecution,
Qu'elle perdesse sa virginitet.	than-she lose her virginity.	Than lose her spiritual purity.
Por o's furet morte a grand honestet.	For this she-would die in grand honour.	For these reasons she died in great honor.
Enz enl fou lo getterent com arde tantost.	Inside in-the fire the they-threw with burn so-quickly.	They threw her into the fire so that she would burn quickly.
Elle colpes non auret, por o no's coist.	She sin not had, for this did-not burn.	She had no sins, for this reason she did not burn.
A czo no's voldret concreidre li rex pagiens;	To this did-not want to-believe the king of-the-pagans;	The pagan king did not want to give in to this;
Ad une spede li roveret tolir lo chieef.	To a sword the order take-off the head.	He ordered her head to be cut off with a sword.
La domnizelle celle kose non contredist:	She damsel this thing not oppose:	The girl did not oppose that idea:
Volt lo seule lazsier si ruovet Krist.	She-wants the earthly-life to-leave thus calls-for Christ.	She wants to abandon earthly life, and she calls upon Christ.
In figure de colomb volat a ciel.	In the-figure of a-dove to-fly to heaven.	In the form of a dove she flew to heaven.

A Brief History of Latin and Romance Languages — *Canticle of Saint Eulalia, 9th Century*

Tuit oram que por nos degnet preier.
Qued avuisset de nos Christus mercit,
Post la mort et a lui nos laist venir,
Par souue clementia.

All to-pray that for our worthy to-pray-for.
Which may-have of our Christ mercy,
After the death and to Him our allow to-come,
By his clemency.

Let us all pray that she will deign to pray for us.
That Christ may have mercy on us,
And may allow us to come to Him after death,
Through His grace.

Word List

Old French	English	Latin
a	in	a
a	in	in
a	to	ad
ad	to	ad
adunet	worships	adoret
amast	to-love	amare
anima	soul	anima
arde	burn	ardere
argent	silver	argentium
auret	had	habebat
auret	had	habet
avuisset	may-have	habuisset
bel	graceful	bellus
bellezour	beautiful	bellatus
buona	good	bona
celle	this	ecce-ille
cels	those	ecce-ille
chi	who	qui
chieef	head	caput
chielt	was-bothered	calere
christiien	Christian (name)	Christianus
Christus	Christ (name)	Christ
ciel	heaven	caelis
clementia	clemency	clementia
coist	burn	coquere
colomb	a-dove	columbus
colpes	sin	culpa
com	with	cum
concreidre	to-believe	concredo
conselliers	counsellers	consiliatores
contredist	oppose	contradictum
corps	body	corpus
cose	thing	causa
czo	this	ecce-hoc

A Brief History of Latin and Romance Languages   *Canticle of Saint Eulalia, 9th Century*

Old French	English	Latin
de	of	de
degnet	worthy	dignitas
Deo	God (name)	Deus
diaule	the-devil	diabolus
dis	days	dies
domnizelle	damsel	*domnicella
dont	but-then	de-inde
e	and	et
element	god	elementum
elle	she	illa
ell'ent	she-then	illa-inde
empedementz	persecution	impedimentum
en	in	in
enimi	enemies	inimicos
enl	in-the	in-ille
enortet	encourages	inhortor
enz	inside	intus
eret	was	erat
eskoltet	listen	auscultare
et	and	et
Eulalia	Eulalia (name)	Eulalia
faire	do	facere
figure	the-figure	figura
fou	fire	focus
fuiet	flee	fugere
furet	she-would	fuerit
fut	was	fuit
getterent	they-threw	iectare
grand	grand	grandis
honestet	honour	honestus
Il	he	ille
in	in	in
kose	thing	causa
Krist	Christ (name)	Christus
la	her	illa
la	she	illa
la	the	illa
la	the	ille
laist	allow	laxare
lazsier	to-leave	laxare
lei	she	illa
les	the	ille
les	the	illi

A Brief History of Latin and Romance Languages   Canticle of Saint Eulalia, 9th Century

Old French	English	Latin
li	her	illa
li	the	ille
lo	the	ille
lo	the	illo
lui	him	ille
maent	resides	remanent
mals	evil	malum
manatce	threats	minacia
Maximiien	Maximian (name)	Maximianus
melz	better	meliorem
menestier	service	ministerium
mercit	mercy	merces
mort	death	mortuus
morte	die	mortuus
ne	nor	nec
ne	not	non
ned	neither	nec
niule	nothing	nihil
nom	name	nomen
non	not	non
nonque	never	nunquam
no'nt	did-not-want	non-volet
nos	our	nostrum
no's	did-not	non-se
o	this	hoc
omque	once	unumque
or	gold	aurum
oram	to-pray	orare
o's	this	illos
pagiens	of-the-pagans	paganus
pagiens	the-pagans	pagani
par	by	per
paramenz	adornments	paramentum
perdesse	lose	perdere
pleier	bend	plicare
polle	girl	puella
por	for	pro
post	after	post
pouret	able	possum
preiement	prayers	precaria
preier	to-pray-for	precari
presentede	presented	praesentem
pulcella	girl	puella

79

A Brief History of Latin and Romance Languages   *Canticle of Saint Eulalia, 9th Century*

Old French	English	Latin
que	that	quid
qued	that	quid
qued	which	quid
qu'elle	than-she	quam-illa
qu'elle	which-she	qui-illa
raneiet	deny	reneget
regiel	regal	regalis
rex	king	rex
roveret	order	rogare
ruovet	calls-for	rogare
sa	her	suus
sempre	always	semper
seruir	serve	servare
seule	earthly-life	solum
si	thus	sic
sostendreiet	she-would-undergo	sustinere
soure	over	super
souue	his	suum
spede	sword	spatha
suon	his	suum
sus	up	subtus
tantost	so-quickly	tantum-tostum
tolir	take-off	tolio
tuit	all	totus
une	a	unum
veintre	kill	vincere
venir	to-come	venire
virginitet	virginity	virginitatem
volat	to-fly	volare
voldrent	wanted	voluerunt
voldret	want	volere
volt	she-wants	volat

Placiti Cassinesi, 10th Century

Old Italian	Literal	English
Sao ko kelle terre, per kelle fini que ki contene, trenta anni le possette parte Sancti Benedicti.	I-know that these lands, by these ends that here contained, thirty years the possession acquired Saint Benedict.	I know that these lands, within the borders shown here, they have been owned by the monastery of St. Benedict for thirty years.
Sao cco kelle terre, per kelle fini que tebe monstrai, Pergoaldi foro, que ki contene, et trenta anni le possette.	I-know that these lands, by these ends that to-you demonstrated, Pergoaldo by-the-court, that who contained, and thirty years the possession.	I know that these lands, within the borders that I have shown you, belonged to Pergoaldo, and he has owned them for thirty years.
Kella terra, per kelle fini que bobe mostrai, sancte Marie è, et trenta anni la posset parte sancte Marie.	This land, by these ends that to-you demonstrated, Saint Mary is, and thirty years the possession acquired Saint Mary.	This land, within the borders that to you are shown, is property of Saint Mary, and the monastery of Saint Mary has owned it for thirty years.
Sao cco kelle terre, per kelle fini que tebe mostrai, trenta anni le possette parte sancte Marie.	I-know that these lands, by these ends that to-you demonstrated, thirty years the posession acquired Saint Mary.	I know those lands, within the borders that I have shown you, they have been owned by the monastery of Saint Mary for thirty years.

Word List

Old Italian	English	Latin
anni	years	anni
Benedicti	Benedict (name)	Benedictus
bobe	to-you	vobis
cco	that	quod
contene	contained	continere
è	is	est
et	and	et
fini	borders	finis
foro	by-the-court	in-foro
kella	this	eccum-illa
kelle	these	eccum-illa
ki	here	qui
ki	who	qui
ko	that	quo
la	the	illa
le	the	ille

A Brief History of Latin and Romance Languages	Placiti Cassinesi, 10th Century

Old Italian	English	Latin
Marie	Mary (name)	Maria
monstrai	demonstrated	monstrum
mostrai	demonstrated	monstrum
parte	acquired	partum
per	by	per
Pergoaldi	Pergoaldo (name)	Pergoaldus
posset	possession	possessio
possette	possession	possessio
que	that	que
sancte	Saint (name)	Sancta
Sancti	Saint (name)	Sancta
sao	I-know	scio
tebe	to-you	tibi
tebe	to-you	tibi
terra	land	terra
terre	lands	terra
trenta	thirty	triginta

Vida of Jaufre Rudel, 13th Century

Old Occitan	Literal	English
Jaufres Rudels de Blaia si fo mout gentils hom, princes de Blaia.	Jaufré Rudel of Blaye so was very noble man, prince of Blaye.	Jaufré Rudel, of Blaye, was a very noble man, prince of Blaye.
Et enamoret se de la comtessa de Tripol, ses vezer, per lo ben qu'el n'auzi dire als pelerins que venguen d'Antiocha.	And enamoured was of the countess of Tripoli, without seeing, by the good which he-heard said by pilgrims who came-from Antioch.	He fell in love with the Countess of Tripoli, without ever having seen her, because of the good things he heard being said about her by pilgrims who came from Antioch.
E fez de leis mains vers ab bons sons, ab paubres motz.	And made of her many verses with good sounds, and simple words.	And he made about her many verses with good melodies but with weak wordings.
E per voluntat de leis vezer, et se croset e se mes en mar, e pres lo malautia en la nau, e fo condug a Tripol, en un alberc, per mort.	And because he-longed of her to-see, and took the-cross and took see-out on the-sea, and fell a sickness on the ship, and was taken to Tripoli, in an inn, near death.	And because he longed to see her, he took up the cross and set out to sail the seas. He fell ill in the ship and was taken to Tripoli, to an inn, near dead.
E fo fait saber a la comtessa et ella venc ad el, al son leit e pres lo antre sos bratz.	And was made known to the countess and she came to him, to his bedside and took him into her arms.	The Countess was notified about him, and she came to him, came right up to his bed, and took him in her arms.
E saup qu'ella era la comtessa, e mantenent recobret l'auzir e·l flairar, e lauzet Dieu, que l'avia la vida sostenguda tro qu'el l'agues vista;	And understood that-she was the countess, and now recovered hearing his smell, and praised God, that he-had the life sustained until that-her had seen;	He recognized that it was the countess, and, instantly, he recovered his sense of hearing and his sense of smell, and he praised God for keeping him alive long enough for him to have the power of vision to see her.
et enaissi el mori entre sos bratz.	and thus he died in her arms.	That is how he died, enfolded in her arms.
Et ella lo fez a gran honor sepellir en la maison del Temple;	And she had made a grand honour buried in the house of Temple;	She had him buried in the house of the Temple, honoring him greatly.
e pois, en aquel dia, ella se rendet morga, per la dolor qu'ella n'ac de la mort de lui.	and then, on that-very day, she went became a-nun, by the pain which-she with-loss of the death of him.	Then she became a nun, that same day, because of the sorrow she felt over his death.

A Brief History of Latin and Romance Languages   Vida of Jaufre Rudel, 13th Century

Word List

Old Occitan	English	Latin
a	a	a
a	to	ad
ab	and	ab
ab	with	apud
ad	to	ad
al	to	ad
alberc	inn	(Germanic)
als	by	illos
antre	into	intro
aquel	that-very	eccum ille
ben	good	bene
Blaia	Blaye (place)	Blavia
bons	good	bonus
bratz	arms	bracchium
comtessa	countess	comitessa
condug	taken	conductus
croset	the-cross	crux
d'Antiocha	Antioch (place)	(Greek)
de	of	de
del	of	de
dia	day	diem
Dieu	God (name)	Deus
dire	said	dixit
dolor	pain	dolorem
e	and	et
e·l	his	ille
el	he	ille
el	him	ille
ella	she	ea
en	in	in
en	on	in
enaissi	thus	ac sic
enamoret	enamoured	enamorat
entre	in	inter
era	was	erat
et	and	et
fait	made	fecit
fez	made	fecit
flairar	smell	flagrare
fo	was	fuit
gentils	noble	gentilis

84

A Brief History of Latin and Romance Languages   Vida of Jaufre Rudel, 13th Century

Old Occitan	English	Latin
gran	grand	grand
hom	man	hominem
honor	honour	honorem
Jaufres	Jaufré (name)	Jaufredus
l'agues	had	abuisset
l'auzir	hearing	audire
l'avia	he-had	habebat
la	the	illa
lauzet	praised	laudat
leis	her	illeius
leit	bedside	lectuo
lo	a	illu
lo	had	illu
lo	him	illu
lo	the	illu
lui	him	illui
mains	many	multi
maison	house	mansionem
malautia	sickness	male habitus
mantenent	now	manus tenir ant
mar	the-sea	mare
mes	see-out	misit
morga	a-nun	monacha
mori	died	mortuus
mort	death	mors
motz	words	muttum
mout	very	multum
n'ac	with-loss	abuit
n'auzi	he-heard	audit
nau	ship	navem
paubres	simple	pauper
pelerins	pilgrims	peregrinus
per	because	per
per	by	per
per	near	per
pois	then	possum
pres	fell	prendere
pres	took	prendere
princes	prince	principe
qu'el	that-her	quod ella
qu'el	which	quod ella
qu'ella	that-she	quod ella
qu'ella	which-she	quod ella

85

A Brief History of Latin and Romance Languages   *Vida of Jaufre Rudel, 13th Century*

Old Occitan	English	Latin
que	that	qui
que	who	qui
recobret	recovered	recuperare
rendet	became	rendere
Rudels	Rudel (name)	(Germanic)
saber	known	sapere
saup	understood	sapere
se	took	se
se	was	se
se	went	se
sepellir	buried	sepulcrum
ses	without	sine
si	so	sic
son	his	suum
sons	sounds	sonorem
sos	her	suum
sostenguda	sustained	sustinere
Temple	Temple (place)	Templum
Tripol	Tripoli (place)	(Greek)
tro	until	entro
un	an	unum
venc	came	venit
venguen	came-from	venit
vers	verses	versum
vezer	seeing	videre
vezer	to-see	videre
vida	life	vita
vista	seen	vista
voluntat	he-longed	voluntat

Vida of Peire d'Alvernhe, 13th Century

Old Occitan	Literal	English
Peire d'Alvernhe si fo de l'evesquat de Clarmon. Savis om fo e ben letratz, e fo filhs dun borges.	Peire d'Alvernhe so was of bishop of Clermont. Clever man was and good letters, and was son of burgher.	Peire d'Alvernhe was a native of the diocese of Clermont. He was a clever and highly educated man and was the son of a burgher.
Bels et avinens fo de la persona, et trobet ben e cantet ben.	Beautiful and comely was of the persona, and composed-poetry good and sang well.	He was of a handsome and comely appearance, and he composed and sang well.
E fo lo primiers bons trobaire que fo outra mon et aquel que fetz los meilhors sons de vers que anc fosson faichs e.l vers que ditz:	And was a first good troubadour than was beyond mountains and that-very than made those best sounds of verses which ever had-been-made made his verses than says:	And he was the first good poet who was every beyond the mountains and the one who made the best music for the verses which ever have been made, and the song that says:
Dejosta ls breus jorns e.ls loncs sers.	Of-while the short days and-the long evenings.	In the season when the days are short and the evenings long.
Canson no fetz neguna, qe non era adoncs negus chantars appellatz cansos, mas vers; ma puois Guirautz de Bornelh fetz la primieira canson que anc fos faita.	Song not made not-one, which not was of-once nor-any song was-called songs, but verses; but then Giraut of Bornelh made the first song than still was made.	He did not compose even one canzone for at that time there was no song called canzone, but only verses; however, later Giraut de Bornelh composed the first canzone tha was ever composed.
Mout fo onratz e grasitz per totz los valens barons que adoncs eran e per totas las valenz dompnas.	Very was honoured and favoured because all those valiant barons than of-once at-that-time and because all those valiant ladies.	He was honoured and favoured by all valiant nobles who were there at that time, and by all valiant ladies.
Et era tengutz per lo meilhor trobador del mon, tro que venc Guirautz de Borneilh.	And was sustained because a better troubadour of-the-world, until than came Giraut of Bourney.	And he was considered the best troubador of the world until Girault de Bornelh came.
Mout se lausava en sos chantars e blasmava los autres trobadors, si qu'el dis de si:	Very himself praised in her songs and blamed those others troubadours, so which this of this:	He praised himself much in his songs and blamed he other troubadours, as such as this:
Peire d'Alvernhe a tal votz	Peire d'Alvernhe has such voice	Peire d'Alvernhe has such a voice
que chanta desobr'e desotz	when singing above-or below	that he sings above or below

A Brief History of Latin and Romance Languages   *Vida of Peire d'Alvernhe, 13th Century*

Old Occitan	Literal	English
e sei so son dous e plazen;	and you-are so yourself before and praise;	even if he praises himself before all others;
e pois es maestre de totz.	and could-be he master of all.	and he could be a master of all,
ab qu'un pauc esclarzis sos motz,	if that-a little he-clarify her words,	if only that he would clarify his words a little,
qu'a penas nulls om los enten.	which unfortunately no man those understand.	since hardly anyone understands them.
Longamen estet et visquet el mon con la bona gen, segon que.m dis lo Dalfins d'Alvernhe, que nasquet en son temps, e puois el fetz penedensa e mori.	Long stayed and lived he me with the good gentle, according-to who-me told the Dauphin of-Auvergne, than was-born in his time, and could he did penance and died.	He stayed there a long time and lived with good honour, according to what the Dauphin of Auvergne who was born at this time told me, and then he did penance and died.

Word List

Old Occitan	English	Latin
a	has	*habet*
ab	if	*ab*
adoncs	of-once	*dunc*
anc	ever	*in-hanc-horam*
anc	still	*in-hanc-horam*
appellatz	was-called	*appellare*
aquel	that-very	*eccum ille*
autres	others	*alterum*
avinens	comely	*advenire*
barons	barons	*baronem*
bels	beautiful	*bellus*
ben	good	*bene*
ben	well	*bene*
blasmava	blamed	*blasphemare*
bona	good	*bonum*
bons	good	*bonus*
borges	burgher	(Germanic)
Borneilh	Bourney (place)	(unknown)
Bornelh	Bornelh (place)	(unknown)
breus	short	*brevis*
canson	song	*cantionem*
cansos	songs	*cantionem*
cantet	sang	*cantat*
chanta	singing	*cantare*
chantars	song	*cantionem*
chantars	songs	*cantionem*

A Brief History of Latin and Romance Languages   *Vida of Peire d'Alvernhe, 13th Century*

Old Occitan	English	Latin
Clarmon	Clermont	Clarus Mons
con	with	cum
Dalfins	Dauphin	dalphinus
d'Alvernhe	d'Alvernhe	Arvernia
d'Alvernhe	of-Auvergne	Arvernia
de	of	de
dejosta	of-while	de-juxta
del	of	de
desobr'e	above-or	de-super
desotz	below	de-subter
dis	this	de-iste
dis	told	dicere
ditz:	says	dicere
dompnas	ladies	dominas
dous	before	dulce
dun	of	de-unum
e	and	et
e.l	his	ille
e.ls	and-the	et is
el	he	ille
en	in	in
enten	understand	intellegentem
era	was	erat
eran	at-that-time	erant
es	he	is
esclarzis	he-clarify	clarificare
estet	stayed	stetit
et	and	et
faichs	made	factus
faita	made	factum
fetz	did	fecit
fetz	made	fecit
filhs	son	filius
fo	was	fuit
fos	was	fuisset
fosson	had-been-made	fuissent
gen	gentle	gens
grasitz	favoured	gratitus
Guirautz	Giraut (name)	Giraudus
is	the	is
jorns	days	diurnum
la	the	illa
las	those	illas

A Brief History of Latin and Romance Languages   *Vida of Peire d'Alvernhe, 13th Century*

Old Occitan	English	Latin
lausava	praised	laudat
letratz	letters	litteratus
l'evesquat	bishop	episcopus
lo	a	illu
lo	the	illu
loncs	long	longue
longamen	long	longa-mente
los	those	illos
ma	but	magis
maestre	master	magister
mas	but	magis
meilhor	better	meliorem
meilhors	best	meliorem
mon	me	meum
mon	mountains	mons
mon	the-world	mundum
mori	died	mortuus
motz	words	muttum
mout	very	multum
nasquet	was-born	natus-est
neguna	not-one	nec-unus
negus	nor-any	nec-ullus
no	not	non
non	not	non
nulls	no	nullus
om	man	hominem
onratz	honoured	honoratus
outra	beyond	ultra
pauc	little	pauculum
Peire	Peire (name)	Petrus
penas	unfortunately	poena
penedensa	penance	paenitentia
per	because	per
persona	persona	persona
plazen	praise	placere
pois	could-be	posse
primieira	first	primus
primiers	first	primus
puois	could	possum
puois	then	possum
qe	which	qui
qu'a	which	quia
que	than	quam

A Brief History of Latin and Romance Languages   Vida of Peire d'Alvernhe, 13ᵗʰ Century

Old Occitan	English	Latin
que	when	quam
que	which	quam
que.m	who-me	qui-me
qu'el	which	qui-ille
qu'un	that-a	qui-unum
savis	clever	sapiens
se	himself	se
segon	according-to	secondum
sei	you-are	essere
sers	evenings	vespers
si	so	si
si:	this	sic
so	so	so
son	his	suum
son	yourself	sunt
sons	sounds	sonorem
sos	her	suum
tal	such	talem
temps	time	tempus
tengutz	sustained	sustinere
totas	all	totus
totz	all	totus
tro	until	entro
trobador	troubadour	*tropatore
trobadors	troubadours	*tropares
trobaire	troubadour	*tropare
trobet	composed-poetry	*tropet
valens	valiant	valere
valenz	valiant	valentina
venc	came	venit
vers	verses	versum
visquet	lived	vivere
votz	voice	vox

Vida of Giraut de Bornelh, 13th Century

Old Occitan	Literal	English
Girautz de Borneill si fo de Limozi, de l'encontrada d'Esiduoill, d'un ric castel del viscomte de Lemoges.	Giraut of Bourney so was of Limoges, of region-encountered Excideuil, of-a rich castle of viscount of Limoges.	Giraut de Borneil was a native of Limousin from the township of Excideuil, from a powerful castle of the vicomte of Limoges.
E fo hom de bas afar, mas savis hom fo de letras e de sen natural.	And was a-man of low affairs, but clever man was of letters and of sense natural.	And he was a man of low class, but a clever and learned man of sound judgement.
E fo meiller trobaire que negus d'aquels qu'eron estat denan ni foron apres lui; per que fo apellatz maestre dels trobadors, et es ancar per toz aquels que ben entendon subtils ditz ni ben pauzatz d'amor ni de sen.	And was better troubadour than nor-any of-anyone who-were existed before or was after him by which was was-called master of-the troubadours and is still by all anyone who well understand subtle sayings either well poetise of-love either of sense.	And he was a better troubadour than any of those who were before or lived after him, therefore he was called master of the troubadours and so he is still for all those who well understand subtle sayings and know how to render words of love and wisdom.
Fort fo honratz per los valenz homes e per los entendenz e per las dompnas qu'entendian los sieus maestrals ditz de las soas chansos.	Strongly was honoured by those valiant men and by those understood and by those ladies who-understood those his masterful words of those his songs.	He was much honoured by the valiant men and by those who understood, and by the ladies who understood his masterly words of his songs.
E la soa vida si era aitals que tot l'invern estava en escola et aprendia letras, e tota la estat anava per cortz e menava ab se dos cantadors que cantavon las soas chansos.	And the his life so was such that all the-winter he-was in school and learning letters, and all the summer he-went by court and lead from him two singers who sang those his songs.	And his life was such that he was at school the whole winter learning, and the whole summer he went from court to court, and with him he took two singers who sang his songs.
Non volc mais muiller, e tot so qu'el gazaingnava dava a sos paubres parenz et a la eglesia de la villa on el nasquet, la quals glesia avia nom, et a ancaras, Saint Gervas.	Not wanted never a-wife, and all so which earned he-gave to his poor parents and to the church of the city in he was-born, the of-which church has name, and of still, Saint Gervaise.	He did not want a wife, ever, and all that he earned, he gave to his poor parents, and to the church of the city in which he was born, which church had and still has today the name of Saint Gervais.
Et aici son escritas gran ren de las soas chansos.	And here his written grand things of those his songs.	And here are written grand things about those songs.

A Brief History of Latin and Romance Languages   Vida of Giraut de Bornelh, 13th Century

Word List

Old Occitan	English	Latin
a	of	a
a	to	ad
ab	from	ab
afar	affairs	ad-facere
aici	here	ad-hicce
aitals	such	eccum-talis
anava	he-went	andare
ancar	still	in-hanc-horam
ancaras	still	in-hanc-horam
apellatz	was-called	appellare
aprendia	learning	apprendere
apres	after	ad-pressum
aquels	anyone	eccum-ille
avia	has	habet
bas	low	bassus
ben	well	bene
Borneill	Bourney (place)	(unknown)
cantadors	singers	cantores
cantavon	sang	cantaverunt
castel	castle	castellum
chansos	songs	cantio
chansos	songs	cantiones
cortz	court	cortem
d'amor	of-love	de-amor
d'aquels	of-anyone	de-eccum-ille
dava	he-gave	dabat
de	of	de
de	of	
del	of	de ille
dels	of-the	de-illos
denan	before	debere
d'Esiduoill	Excideuil (place)	Exidolium
ditz	sayings	dicere
ditz	words	dicere
dompnas	ladies	dominas
dos	two	duo
d'un	of-a	de unum
e	and	et
eglesia	church	ecclesia
el	he	ille
en	in	in

93

A Brief History of Latin and Romance Languages   *Vida of Giraut de Bornelh, 13th Century*

Old Occitan	English	Latin
entendenz	understood	intendere
entendon	understand	intendere
era	was	erat
es	is	est
escola	school	scholam
escritas	written	scriptum
estat	existed	status
estat	summer	aestas
estava	he-was	is-erat
et	and	and
et	and	et
fo	was	fuit
foron	was	fuit
fort	strongly	fortis
gazaingnava	earned	(Germanic)
Gervas	Gervaise (name)	Gervasius
Girautz	Giraut (name)	Giraudus
glesia	church	ecclesia
gran	grand	grandis
hom	a-man	hominem
hom	man	hominem
homes	men	homines
honratz	honoured	honoratus
la	the	illa
las	those	illas
Lemoges	Limoges (place)	Lemovicinus
l'encontrada	region-encountered	regio-incontrata
letras	letters	littera
letras	letters	litteras
Limozi	Limoges (place)	Lemovicinus
l'invern	the-winter	hibernus
los	those	illos
lui;	him	ille
maestrals	masterful	magistralis
maestre	master	magister
mais	never	non-venit-magis
mas	but	magis
meiller	better	meliorem
menava	lead	minare
muiller	a-wife	mulierem
nasquet	was-born	natus-est
natural	natural	naturalem
negus	nor-any	nec-ullus

A Brief History of Latin and Romance Languages   Vida of Giraut de Bornelh, 13ᵗʰ Century

Old Occitan	English	Latin
ni	either	nec
ni	or	nec
nom	name	nominem
non	not	non
on	in	de-unde
parenz	parents	parentem
paubres	poor	poveres
pauzatz	poetise	poeta
per	by	per
quals	of-which	qua-illos
que	than	quam
que	that	qui
que	which	quid
que	who	qui
qu'el	which	qui-ille
qu'entendian	who-understood	qui-intendere
qu'eron	who-were	quam-erunt
ren	things	rem
ric	rich	(Germanic)
Saint	Saint (name)	Sanctus
savis	clever	sapere
se	him	se
sen	sense	(Germanic)
si	so	si
si	so	sic
sieus	his	se-illus
so	so	si
soa	his	sua
soas	his	se-illos
soas	his	suos
soas	his	suus
son	his	suus
sos	his	suus
subtils	subtle	subtilis
tot	all	totus
tota	all	totus
toz	all	totus
trobadors	troubadours	*tropares
trobaire	troubadour	*tropare
valenz	valiant	valentina
vida	life	vita
villa	city	villa
viscomte	viscount	vicecomes

A Brief History of Latin and Romance Languages   *Vida of Giraut de Bornelh, 13th Century*

Old Occitan   *English*   *Latin*

volc   wanted   *voluit*

Cantigas de Santa María, 13th Century

Old Galician-Portuguese	Literal	English
Esta é de loor.	This is of praise.	This is a song of praise.
Santa María,	Saint Maria,	Holy Mary,
Strela do día,	Star of day,	Star of Day,
móstra-nos vía	show-us the-way	show us the way
pera Déus e nos guía.	to God and us guide.	to God and be our guide.
Ca veer faze-los errados	Because to-see make-those mistaken	You make the wayward,
que perder foran per pecados	who lost they-were because-of sin	who were lost because of sin,
entender de que mui culpados	understand of who very guilty	see and understand that they are very guilty.
son; mais per ti son perdõados	they-are; but by you they pardoned	But they are pardoned by you
da ousadía	for boldness	for the temerity
que lles fazía	which them made	which caused them
fazer folía	made reckless	recklessly to do
mais que non devería.	but what not should.	what they should not.
Amostrar- nos deves carreira	Show us you-must the-path	You must show us the way
por gãar en toda maneira	for to-win in all	in all our deeds to win
a sen par luz e verdadeira	of without match light and truth	the true and matchless light
que tu dar- nos pódes senlleira;	which you give us can singularly;	which only you can give us,
ca Déus a ti a	because God of you to	for God would
outorgaría	bestow	grant it to you,
e a querría	and of willingly	and most willingly
por ti dar e daría.	for your give of giving.	bestow it for your sake.
Guïar ben nos pód' o téu siso	Guide well us can the of-you sense	Your wisdom can guide us far better
mais ca ren pera Paraíso	but because nothing because Paradise	than any other thing to Paradise,
u Déus ten sempre goi' e riso	where God has always joy and delight	where God has always delight and joy
pora quen en el creer quiso;	for whoever in him believe seeks;	for whoever would believe in Him.
e prazer-m-ía	I should-rejoice	I should rejoice
se te prazía	if you pleases	if it please you
que foss' a mía	that to-have-been that my	to let my
alm' en tal companñía.	soul in such company.	soul be in such company.

A Brief History of Latin and Romance Languages   *Cantigas de Santa María, 13th Century*

Word List

Old Galician-Portuguese	English	Latin
a	of	a
a	that	a
a	to	ad
alm'	soul	anima
amostrar-	show	monstrare
ben	well	bene
ca	because	quia
carreira	the-path	carraria
compannía	company	*compania
creer	believe	credere
culpados	guilty	cupla
da	for	de
dar	give	dare
dar-	give	dare
daría	giving	dare
de	of	de
Déus	God (name)	Deus
debería	should	debere
deves	you-must	debere
día	day	diem
do	of	de
e	and	et
e	I	ego
e	of	e
é	is	est
el	him	ille
en	in	in
entender	understand	intendere
errados	mistaken	erratus
esta	this	iste
faze-los	make-those	facere-illos
fazer	made	faciem
fazía	made	faciem
folía	reckless	follis
foran	they-were	foran
foss'	to-have-been	fuisse
gãar	to-win	ganare
goi'	joy	gaudia
guía	guide	(Germanic)
guïar	guide	(Germanic)
lles	them	illos
loor	praise	laudare
luz	light	lux

A Brief History of Latin and Romance Languages   *Cantigas de Santa María, 13th Century*

mais	but	magis
maneira	deeds	manuaria
María	Maria (name)	Maria
mía	my	mea
móstra-nos	show-us	demonstrare-nos
mui	very	multum
non	not	non
nos	us	nos
o	the	ille
ousadía	boldness	audere
outorgaría	bestow	auctoricare
par	match	parallelus
paraíso	paradise	paradisum
pecados	sin	peccatum
per	because-of	per
per	by	per
pera	because	per
pera	to	per
perder	lost	perdere
perdõados	pardoned	perdonare
pód'	can	posse
pódes	can	posse
por	for	per
pora	for	per
prazer-m-ía	should-rejoice	placere
prazía	pleases	placere
que	that	qui
que	what	qui
que	which	qui
que	who	qui
quen	whoever	quem
querría	willingly	quaero
quiso	seeks	quaero
ren	nothing	res-nata
riso	delight	risus
Santa	Saint (name)	Sancta
se	if	si
sempre	always	semper
sen	without	sine
senlleira	singularly	singularis
siso	sense	sensus
son	they	sunt
son	they-are	sunt
strela	star	stella
tal	such	talis
te	you	te
ten	has	tenere

99

A Brief History of Latin and Romance Languages   *Cantigas de Santa María, 13th Century*

téu	of-you	tui
ti	you	te
ti	your	te
toda	all	totus
tu	you	te
u	where	ubi
veer	to-see	videre
verdadeira	truth	veritatem
vía	the-way	via

Cantico Delle Creature, 13th Century

Italian	Literal	English
Altissimu, onnipotente, bon Signore,	The-highest, almighty, good Lord,	Most high, almighty, good lord,
tue so' le laude, la gloria e 'honore et onne benedictione.	yours are' the praises, the glory and 'honour and every blessing.	yours are the praises, the glory, the honour, and all blessing.
Ad te solo, Altissimo, se konfàno	To you alone, The-highest, they belong	To you alone, most high, do they belong
et nullu homo ène dignu te mentovare.	and no man is worthy you mentioning.	and no man is worthy of mentioning you.
Laudato sie, mi' Signore, cum tucte le tue creature,	Praise be, my' Lord, with all the your creatures,	Be praised, my Lord, with all your creatures,
spetialmente messor lo frate sole,	especially the-harvester the brother sun,	especially the harvester, the brother sun,
lo qual è iorno, et allumini noi per lui.	this which is the-day, and the-light ours because-of him.	of which the day and the light is ours because of him.
Et ellu è bellu e radiante cum grande splendore,	And he is beautiful and radiant with grand splendour,	And he is beautiful and radiant with grand splendour,
de te, Altissimo, porta significatione.	of you, The-highest, brings signification.	of you, most high, he bears the sign.
Laudato si', mi' Signore, per sora luna e le stelle,	Praise be, my' Lord, through Sister Moon and the stars,	Be praised, my lord, for sister moon and the stars;
in celu l'ài formate clarite et pretiose et belle.	in heaven you-have formed clearly and preciously and beautiful.	in the heavens you have made them clear, precious and beautiful.
Laudato si', mi' Signore, per frate vento	Praise be, my' Lord, through Brother Wind	Be praised, my lord, for brother wind
et per aere et nubilo et sereno et onne tempo,	and through the-air and the-clouds and serene and all weather,	and for the air and the clouds, and all serene weather,
per lo quale a le tue creature dài sustentamento.	by this which is the you creatures given sustenance.	by which you give your creatures sustenance.
Laudato si', mi' Signore, per sor' aqua,	Praise be, my' Lord, through Sister' Water,	Be praised, my Lord, through sister water;
la quale è multo utile et humile et pretiosa et casta.	the which is much useful and humble and precious and pure.	which is very useful and humble and precious and pure.
Laudato si', mi' Signore, per frate focu,	Praise be, my' Lord, through Brother Fire,	Be praised, my Lord, through brother fire,
per lo quale ennallumini la nocte,	for is which illuminates the night,	through whom you brighten the night,
et ello è bello et iocundo et robustoso et forte.	and he is handsome and playful and robust and strong.	and he is handsome and cheerful, and robust and strong.
Laudato si', mi' Signore, per sora nostra matre terra,	Praise be, my' Lord, through sister ours Mother Earth,	Be praised, my lord, through our sister mother earth,
la quale ne sustenta et governa,	this which us sustains and maintains,	who sustains us and maintains us,
et produce diversi fructi con coloriti flori et herba.	and produces diverse fruits with coloured flowers and herbs.	and produces diverse fruits with coloured flowers and herbs.

A Brief History of Latin and Romance Languages   *Cantico Delle Creature, 13th Century*

Italian	Literal	English
Laudato si', mi' Signore, per quelli ke perdonano per lo tuo amore,	Praise be, my' Lord, through those who pardon through the your love,	Be praised, my lord, through those who forgive for the love of you;
et sostengo infirmitate et tribulatione.	and endure infirmity and tribulation.	through those who endure sickness and tribulation.
Beati quelli che 'l sosterrano in pace,	Blessed those who 'the endure in peace,	Blessed be those who endure in peace,
ca da te, Altissimo, sirano incoronati.	as from you, The-highest, they-will-be crowned.	for by you, most high, they will be crowned.
Laudato si' mi' Signore per sora nostra morte corporale,	Praise be' my' Lord through sister ours death of-the-body,	Be praised, my lord, through our sister bodily death,
da la quale nullu homo vivente pò scappare:	of the which no man living may escape:	from which no man living can escape.
guai a quelli che morrano ne le peccata mortali;	woe to those who die while the sin mortal;	woe to those who die while in mortal sin
beati quelli che trovarà ne le tue santissime voluntati,	blessed those who find while the your sacred will,	blessed are those who are found while doing your sacred will,
ka la morte secunda no 'l farrà male.	that the death following not 'the bring harm.	that the second death will not bring harm.
Laudate et benedicete mi' Signore' et ringratiate	Praise and blessed my' Lord' and thanks-to-you	Praise and bless my lord and give thanks
et serviateli cum grande humilitate.	and serve with grand humility.	and serve with grand humility.

Word List

Old Italian	English	Latin
a	is	*a*
a	to	*a*
ad	to	*ad*
aere	the-air	*aerem*
allumini	the-light	*luminis*
altissimo	the-highest	*altissimus*
altissimu	the-highest	*altissimus*
amore	love	*amor*
aqua	water	*aqua*
beati	blessed	*beati*
belle	beautiful	*bellus*
bello	handsome	*bellus*
bellu	beautiful	*bellus*
benedicete	bless	*benedire*
benedictione	blessing	*benedire*
bon	good	*bonus*
ca	as	*quia*
casta	pure	*castus*

A Brief History of Latin and Romance Languages   *Cantico Delle Creature, 13th Century*

Old Italian	English	Latin
celu	heaven	caelus
che	who	qui
clarite	clearly	claritate
coloriti	coloured	color
con	with	cum
corporale	of-the-body	corporalem
creature	creatures	creatura
cum	with	cum
da	from	de
da	of	de
dài	given	dare
de	of	de
dignu	worthy	dignus
diversi	diverse	diversus
e	and	e
è	is	est
ello	he	ille
ellu	he	ille
ène	is	est
ennallumini	illuminates	luminis
et	and	et
farrà	bring	fero
flori	flowers	florae
focu	fire	focus
formate	formed	formare
forte	strong	forte
frate	brother	frater
fructi	fruits	fructus
gloria	glory	gloria
governa	maintains	gubernare
grande	grand	grande
guai	woe	vae
herba	herbs	herba
homo	man	homo
honore	honour	honor
humile	humble	humile
humilitate	humility	humilitas
in	in	in
incoronati	crowned	incoronare
infirmitate	infirmity	infirmitas
iocundo	playful	iucundus
iorno	the-day	diurnus
ka	that	qua

A Brief History of Latin and Romance Languages   *Cantico Delle Creature, 13th Century*

Old Italian	English	Latin
ke	who	quo
konfàno	belong	confinis
l	the	ille
la	the	illa
la	this	illa
l'ài	you-have	te habes
laudate	praise	laudate
laudato	praise	laudato
laude	praises	laudat
le	the	ille
lo	is	lo
lo	the	lo
lo	this	lo
lui	him	illui
luna	moon	luna
male	harm	male
matre	mother	mater
mentovare	mentioning	mente habere
messor	the-harvester	messor
mi	my	mi
morrano	die	morientur
mortali	mortal	mortalem
morte	death	mortem
multo	much	multo
ne	us	inde
ne	while	inde
no	not	non
nocte	night	noctem
noi	ours	nos
nostra	ours	nostra
nubilo	the-clouds	nubilo
nullu	no	nullus
onne	all	omne
onne	every	omne
onnipotente	almighty	omnipotentem
pace	peace	pax
peccata	sin	peccatum
per	because-of	per
per	by	per
per	through	per
perdonano	pardon	perdonare
pò	may	potest
porta	brings	portare

A Brief History of Latin and Romance Languages   *Cantico Delle Creature, 13th Century*

Old Italian	English	Latin
pretiosa	precious	pretiosus
pretiose	preciously	pretiosus
produce	produces	productus
qual	which	qualis
quale	which	quale
quelli	those	eccum ille
radiante	radiant	radians
ringratiate	give-thanks	gratia
robustoso	robust	robustus
santissime	sacred	sanctissime
scappare	escape	excappare
se	they	eae
secunda	following	secundus
sereno	serene	serenus
serviateli	serve	servare
si	be	si
si'	be	esse
sie	be	esse
significatione	signification	significatio
signore	lord	seniorem
sirano	they-will-be	erunt
so	are	sunt
sole	sun	sol
solo	alone	solus
sor	sister	soror
sora	sister	soror
sostengo	endure	sustinere
sosterrano	endure	sustinere
spetialmente	especially	specialis
splendore	splendour	splendor
stelle	stars	stella
sustenta	sustains	sustinere
sustentamento	sustenance	sustinere
te	you	te
tempo	weather	tempus
terra	earth	terra
tribulatione	tribulation	tribulatio
trovarà	find	tropare
tucte	all	totus
tue	you	tu
tue	your	tuum
tue	yours	tuum
tuo	your	tuum

A Brief History of Latin and Romance Languages *Cantico Delle Creature, 13th Century*

Old Italian	English	*Latin*
utile	useful	*utile*
vento	wind	*venti*
vivente	living	*vivens*
voluntati	will	*voluntas*

English to Old French

English	Old French	English	Old French

A, a

a	*une*		
able	*pouret*		
adornments	*paramenz*		
a-dove	*colomb*		
after	*post*		
against	*contra*		
aid	*adiudha, aiudha*		
all	*tuit*		
allow	*laist*		
always	*sempre*		
am-able	*pois*		
a-man	*om*		
and	*e, et*		
as	*cum*		

B, b

beautiful	*bellezour*
bend	*pleier*
better	*melz*
body	*corps*
breaks	*fraint*
brother	*fradra, fradre*
burn	*arde, coist*
but-then	*dont*
by	*par, per*

C, c

calls-for	*ruovet*
Charles (name)	*Karle, Karlo, Karlus*
Christ (name)	*Christus, Krist*
christian	*christian*
Christian (name)	*christiien*
clemency	*clementia*
common	*commun*
council	*plaid*
counsellers	*conselliers*

D, d

damnation	*damno*
damsel	*domnizelle*
day	*di*
days	*dis*
death	*mort*
deny	*raneiet*
did-not	*no's*
did-not-want	*no'nt*
die	*morte*
dissuade	*returnar*
do	*faire*

E, e

earthly-life	*seule*
encourages	*enortet*
enemies	*enimi*
Eulalia (name)	*Eulalia*
every	*cadhuna*
evil	*mals*

F, f

fire	*fou*
flee	*fuiet*
for	*por, Pro*
future	*auant*

G, g

girl	*polle, pulcella*
gives	*dunat*
god	*element*
God (name)	*Deo, Deo, Deus*
gold	*or*
good	*buona*

English	Old French
graceful	bel
grand	grand

H, h

English	Old French
had	auret, auret
he	il
head	chieef
heaven	ciel
her	la, li, sa
him	lui
him-from	int, l'int
his	son, souue, suo, suon
honour	honestet
how-much	quant

I, i

English	Old French
I	eo, io, ju
if	si
in	a, a, en, in
inside	enz
in-so-far-as	o
in-the	enl
in-to	in
it	lo

K, k

English	Old French
keeps	conservat
kill	veintre
king	rex

L, l

English	Old French
likewise	altresi
listen	eskoltet
lord	sendra
lose	perdesse
Lothair (name)	Ludher
Louis (name)	Lodhuuigs, Lodhuuuig

M, m

English	Old French
Maximian (name)	Maximiien
may-be	sit
may-have	avuisset
me	me
mercy	mercit
mine	meos
my	meon

N, n

English	Old French
name	nom
neither	ne, ned
never	nonque, nunquam
no	nulla
no-one	neuls
nor	ne
not	ne, non, nul, nun
nothing	niule

O, o

English	Old French
of	de
of-the-pagans	pagiens
of-this	d'ist
once	omque
oppose	contredist
order	roveret
our	nos, nostro
over	soure

P, p

English	Old French
part	part
persecution	empedementz
power	podir
prayers	preiement
presented	presentede

R, r

A Brief History of Latin and Romance Languages

English to Old French

English	Old French	English	Old French
regal	*regiel*	to	*a, ad*
resides	*maent*	to-believe	*concreidre*
right	*dreit*	to-come	*venir*
		to-fly	*volat*
		to-him	*li*
		to-leave	*lazsier*
		to-love	*amast*
		to-me	*mi*
		to-pray	*oram*
		to-pray-for	*preier*
		to-protect	*saluar*
		to-this	*cist*

S, s

English	Old French
sacrament	*sagrament*
salvation	*saluament*
serve	*seruir*
service	*menestier*
shall-do	*fazet*
shall-take	*prindrai*
she	*elle, la, lei*
she-then	*ell'ent*
she-wants	*volt*
she-would	*furet*
she-would-undergo	*sostendreiet*
should	*dist*
silver	*argent*
sin	*colpes*
so	*si*
so-quickly	*tantost*
soul	*anima*
sword	*spede*
sworn	*iurat*

U, u

English	Old French
up	*sus*

V, v

English	Old French
virginity	*virginitet*

W, w

English	Old French
want	*voldret*
wanted	*voldrent*
was	*eret, fut*
was-bothered	*chielt*
which	*que, qued, qui*
which-she	*qu'elle*
who	*chi, cui*
will	*uol*
will-be	*er*
will-protect	*saluarai*
wisdom	*sauir*
with	*ab, com*
worships	*adunet*
worthy	*degnet*

T, t

English	Old French
take-off	*tolir*
than-she	*qu'elle*
that	*que, qued, quid*
the	*la, la, les, les, li, lo, lo*
the-devil	*diaule*
the-figure	*figure*
the-love-of	*amur*
the-pagans	*pagiens*
the-people	*poblo*
they-threw	*getterent*
thing	*cosa, cose, kose*
this	*celle, czo, o, o's*
those	*cels*
threats	*manatce*
thus	*si*

English to Old Galician-Portuguese

English	Old Galician-Portuguese	English	Old Galician-Portuguese

A, a

all	*toda*
always	*sempre*
and	*e*

B, b

because	*ca, pera*
because-of	*per*
believe	*creer*
bestow	*outorgaría*
boldness	*ousadía*
but	*mais*
by	*per*

C, c

| can | *pód', pódes* |
| company | *compannía* |

D, d

day	*día*
deeds	*maneira*
delight	*riso*

F, f

| for | *da, por, pora* |

G, g

give	*dar, dar-*
giving	*daría*
God (name)	*Déus*
guide	*guía, guïar*

| guilty | *culpados* |

H, h

| has | *ten* |
| him | *el* |

I, i

I	*e*
if	*se*
in	*en*
is	*é*

J, j

| joy | *goi'* |

K, k

L, l

| light | *luz* |
| lost | *perder* |

M, m

made	*fazer, fazía*
make-those	*faze-los*
Maria (name)	*María*
match	*par*
mistaken	*errados*
my	*mía*

N, n

A Brief History of Latin and Romance Languages

English	Old Galician-Portuguese
not	*non*
nothing	*ren*

O, o

English	Old Galician-Portuguese
of	*a, de, do, e*
of-you	*téu*

P, p

English	Old Galician-Portuguese
paradise	*paraíso*
pardoned	*perdõados*
pleases	*prazía*
praise	*loor*

R, r

English	Old Galician-Portuguese
reckless	*folía*

S, s

English	Old Galician-Portuguese
Saint (name)	*Santa*
seeks	*quiso*
sense	*siso*
should	*devería*
should-rejoice	*prazer-m-ía*
show	*amostrar-*
show-us	*móstra-nos*
sin	*pecados*
singularly	*senlleira*
soul	*alm'*
star	*strela*
such	*tal*

T, t

English	Old Galician-Portuguese
that	*a, que*
the	*o*
them	*lles*
the-path	*carreira*

English to Old Galician-Portuguese

English	Old Galician-Portuguese
the-way	*vía*
they	*son*
they-are	*son*
they-were	*foran*
this	*esta*
to	*a, pera*
to-have-been	*foss'*
to-see	*veer*
to-win	*gãar*
truth	*verdadeira*

U, u

English	Old Galician-Portuguese
understand	*entender*
us	*nos*

V, v

English	Old Galician-Portuguese
very	*mui*

W, w

English	Old Galician-Portuguese
well	*ben*
what	*que*
where	*u*
which	*que*
who	*que*
whoever	*quen*
willingly	*querría*
without	*sen*

Y, y

English	Old Galician-Portuguese
you	*te, ti, tu*
you-must	*deves*
your	*ti*

English to Old Italian

English	Old Italian

A, a

acquired	*parte*
all	*onne, tucte*
almighty	*onnipotente*
alone	*solo*
and	*e, et*
are	*so*
as	*ca*
a-white	*albo*

B, b

be	*si, si', sie*
beautiful	*belle, bellu*
because-of	*per*
belong	*konfàno*
Benedict (name)	*Benedicti*
black	*negro*
bless	*benedicete*
blessed	*beati*
blessing	*benedictione*
borders	*fini*
bring	*farrà*
brings	*porta*
brother	*frate*
by	*per*
by-the-court	*foro*

C, c

clearly	*clarite*
coloured	*coloriti*
contained	*contene*
creatures	*creature*
crowned	*incoronati*

D, d

death	*morte*
demonstrated	*monstrai, mostrai*
die	*morrano*
diverse	*diversi*

E, e

earth	*terra*
endure	*sostengo, sosterrano*
escape	*scappare*
especially	*spetialmente*
every	*onne*

F, f

fields	*pratalia*
find	*trovarà*
fire	*focu*
flowers	*flori*
following	*secunda*
formed	*formate*
from	*da*
fruits	*fructi*

G, g

given	*dài*
give-thanks	*ringratiate*
glory	*gloria*
good	*bon*
grand	*grande*

H, h

handsome	*bello*
harm	*male*
he	*ello, ellu, se*
heaven	*celu*
he-held	*teneba*

A Brief History of Latin and Romance Languages   English to Old Italian

English	Old Italian
he-plowed	araba
herbs	herba
here	ki
he-sowed	seminaba
him	lui
honour	honore
humble	humile
humility	humilitate

I, i

English	Old Italian
I-know	sao
illuminates	ennallumini
in	in
infirmity	infirmitate
is	a, è, ène, lo

L, l

English	Old Italian
land	terra
lands	terre
led	pareba
living	vivente
lord	signore
love	amore

M, m

English	Old Italian
maintains	governa
man	homo
Mary (name)	Marie
may	pò
mentioning	mentovare
moon	luna
mortal	mortali
mother	matre
much	multo
my	mi

N, n

English	Old Italian
night	nocte
no	nullu
not	no, non

O, o

English	Old Italian
of	da, de
of-the-body	corporale
ours	noi, nostra
out-of	ab
oxen	boves

P, p

English	Old Italian
pardon	perdonano
peace	pace
Pergoaldo (name)	Pergoaldi
playful	iocundo
plough	versorio
possession	posset, possette
praise	laudate, laudato
praises	laude
precious	pretiosa
preciously	pretiose
produces	produce
pure	casta

R, r

English	Old Italian
radiant	radiante
robust	robustoso

S, s

English	Old Italian
sacred	santissime
Saint (name)	sancte, Sancti
secrets	secrita
seed	semen
serene	sereno
serve	serviateli
signification	significatione
sin	peccata
sister	sor, sora

A Brief History of Latin and Romance Languages   *English to Old Italian*

English	Old Italian
splendour	*splendore*
stars	*stelle*
strong	*forte*
sun	*sole*
sustains	*sustenta*
sustenance	*sustentamento*

T, t

English	Old Italian
that	*cco, ka, ko, que*
the	*ille, l, la, le, lo*
the-air	*aere*
the-clouds	*nubilo*
the-day	*iorno*
the-harvester	*messor*
the-highest	*altissimo, altissimu*
the-light	*allumini*
the-mouth	*boce*
these	*kelle*
they	*se*
they-will-be	*sirano*
thirty	*trenta*
this	*kella, la, lo*
those	*quelli*
through	*per*
to	*a, ad*
to-speak	*dicere*
to-you	*bobe, tebe*
tribulation	*tribulatione*

U, u

English	Old Italian
us	*ne*
useful	*utile*

W, w

English	Old Italian
water	*aqua*
weather	*tempo*
which	*qual, quale*
while	*ne*
white	*alba*
who	*che, ke, ki*

English	Old Italian
will	*voluntati*
wind	*vento*
with	*con, cum*
woe	*guai*
worthy	*dignu*

Y, y

English	Old Italian
years	*anni*
you	*te, tue*
you-have	*l'ài*
your	*tue, tuo*
yours	*tue*

English to Old Occitan

English	Old Occitan

A, a

a	a, lo
above-or	desobr'e
according-to	segon
affairs	afar
after	apres
all	tot, tota, totas, totz, toz
a-man	hom
an	un
and	ab, e, et, et
and-the	e.ls
Antioch (place)	d'Antiocha
a-nun	morga
anyone	aquels
arms	bratz
at-that-time	eran
a-wife	muiller

B, b

barons	barons
beautiful	bels
became	rendet
because	per
bedside	leit
before	denan, dous
below	desotz
best	meilhors
better	meilhor, meiller
beyond	outra
bishop	l'evesquat
blamed	blasmava
Blaye (place)	Blaia
Bornelh (place)	Bornelh
Bourney (place)	Borneilh, Borneill
burgher	borges
buried	sepellir
but	ma, mas
by	als, per

C, c

came	venc
came-from	venguen
castle	castel
church	eglesia, glesia
city	villa
Clermont	Clarmon
clever	savis, savis
comely	avinens
composed-poetry	trobet
could	puois
could-be	pois
countess	comtessa
court	cortz

D, d

d'Alvernhe	d'Alvernhe
Dauphin	Dalfins
day	dia
days	jorns
death	mort
did	fetz
died	mori

E, e

earned	gazaingnava
either	ni
enamoured	enamoret
evenings	sers
ever	anc
Excideuil (place)	d'Esiduoill
existed	estat

F, f

115

A Brief History of Latin and Romance Languages   English to Old Occitan

English	Old Occitan
favoured	*grasitz*
fell	*pres*
first	*primieira, primiers*
from	*ab*

G, g

English	Old Occitan
gentle	*gen*
Gervaise (name)	*Gervas*
Giraut (name)	*Girautz, Guirautz*
God (name)	*Dieu*
good	*ben, bona, bons*
grand	*gran, gran*

H, h

English	Old Occitan
had	*l'agues, lo*
had-been-made	*fosson*
has	*a, avia*
he	*el, es*
hearing	*l'auzir*
he-clarify	*esclarzis*
he-gave	*dava*
he-had	*l'avia*
he-heard	*n'auzi*
he-longed	*voluntat*
her	*leis, sos*
here	*aici*
he-was	*estava*
he-went	*anava*
him	*el, lo, lui, lui;, se*
himself	*se*
his	*e.l, e·l, sieus, soa, soas, soas, soas, son, son, sos*
honour	*honor*
honoured	*honratz, onratz*
house	*maison*

I, i

English	Old Occitan
if	*ab*
in	*en, entre, on*

English	Old Occitan
inn	*alberc*
into	*antre*
is	*es*

J, j

English	Old Occitan
Jaufré (name)	*Jaufres*

K, k

English	Old Occitan
known	*saber*

L, l

English	Old Occitan
ladies	*dompnas*
lead	*menava*
learning	*aprendia*
letters	*letras, letras, letratz*
life	*vida*
Limoges (place)	*Lemoges, Limozi*
little	*pauc*
lived	*visquet*
long	*loncs, longamen*
low	*bas*

M, m

English	Old Occitan
made	*faichs, fait, faita, fetz, fez*
man	*hom, om*
many	*mains*
master	*maestre*
masterful	*maestrals*
me	*mon*
men	*homes*
mountains	*mon*

N, n

English	Old Occitan
name	*nom*
natural	*natural*
near	*per*

A Brief History of Latin and Romance Languages English to Old Occitan

English	Old Occitan
never	*mais*
no	*nulls*
noble	*gentils*
nor-any	*negus*
not	*no, non*
not-one	*neguna*
now	*mantenent*

O, o

English	Old Occitan
of	*a, de, de, del, del, dun*
of-a	*d'un*
of-anyone	*d'aquels*
of-Auvergne	*d'Alvernhe*
of-love	*d'amor*
of-once	*adoncs*
of-the	*dels*
of-which	*quals*
of-while	*dejosta*
on	*en*
or	*ni*
others	*autres*

P, p

English	Old Occitan
pain	*dolor*
parents	*parenz*
Peire (name)	*Peire*
penance	*penedensa*
persona	*persona*
pilgrims	*pelerins*
poetise	*pauzatz*
poor	*paubres*
praise	*plazen*
praised	*lausava, lauzet*
prince	*princes*

R, r

English	Old Occitan
recovered	*recobret*
region-encountered	*l'encontrada*
rich	*ric*
Rudel (name)	*Rudels*

S, s

English	Old Occitan
said	*dire*
Saint (name)	*Saint*
sang	*cantavon, cantet*
sayings	*ditz*
says	*ditz:*
school	*escola*
seeing	*vezer*
seen	*vista*
see-out	*mes*
sense	*sen*
she	*ella*
ship	*nau*
short	*breus*
sickness	*malautia*
simple	*paubres*
singers	*cantadors*
singing	*chanta*
smell	*flairar*
so	*si, si, so, so*
son	*filhs*
song	*canson, chantars*
songs	*cansos, chansos, chansos, chantars*
sounds	*sons*
stayed	*estet*
still	*anc, ancar, ancaras*
strongly	*fort*
subtle	*subtils*
such	*aitals, tal*
summer	*estat*
sustained	*sostenguda, tengutz*

T, t

English	Old Occitan
taken	*condug*
Temple (place)	*Temple*
than	*que*
that	*que*
that-a	*qu'un*
that-her	*qu'el*
that-she	*qu'ella*

A Brief History of Latin and Romance Languages English to Old Occitan

English	Old Occitan
that-very	aquel
the	is, la, lo
the-cross	croset
then	pois, puois
the-sea	mar
the-winter	l'invern
the-world	mon
things	ren
this	dis, si:
those	las, los
thus	enaissi
time	temps
to	a, ad, al
told	dis
took	pres, se
to-see	vezer
Tripoli (place)	Tripol
troubadour	trobador, trobaire
troubadours	trobadors
two	dos

U, u

English	Old Occitan
understand	enten, entendon
understood	entendenz, saup
unfortunately	penas
until	tro

V, v

English	Old Occitan
valiant	valens, valenz
verses	vers
very	mout
viscount	viscomte
voice	votz

W, w

English	Old Occitan
wanted	volc
was	era, fo, foron, fos, se
was-born	nasquet
was-called	apellatz, appellatz
well	ben

English	Old Occitan
went	se
when	que
which	qe, qu'el, qu'a, que, que, qu'el
which-she	qu'ella
who	que
who-me	que.m
who-understood	qu'entendian
who-were	qu'eron
with	ab, con
with-loss	n'ac
without	ses
words	ditz, motz
written	escritas

Y, y

English	Old Occitan
you-are	sei
yourself	son

Latin to Old French

Latin	Old French	Latin	Old French

A, a

Latin	Old French
a	a
ab	ab
ab-ante	auant
ad	a, ad
adiuto	adiudha, aiudha
adoret	adunet
alter-si	altresi
amare	amast
amor	amur
anima	anima
ardere	arde
argentium	argent
aurum	or
auscultare	eskoltet

B, b

Latin	Old French
bellatus	bellezour
bellus	bel
bona	buona

C, c

Latin	Old French
caelis	ciel
calere	chielt
caput	chieef
Carolus	Karle, Karlo, Karlus
catunum	cadhuna
causa	cosa, cose, kose
Christ	Christus
christianus	christian, christiien
Christus	Krist
clementia	clementia
columbus	colomb
communitas	commun
concredo	concreidre
conservare	conservat
consiliatores	conselliers

Latin	Old French
contra	contra
contradictum	contredist
coquere	coist
corpus	corps
culpa	colpes
cum	com, cum

D, d

Latin	Old French
damnatio	damno
de	de
de-inde	dont
de-iste	dist, d'ist
Deo	Deo
Deus	Deo, Deus
diabolus	diaule
diem	di
dies	dis
dignitas	degnet
directus	dreit
donat	dunat

E, e

Latin	Old French
ecce-hoc	czo
ecce-ille	celle, cels
ecce-iste	cist
ego	eo, io, ju
elementum	element
erat	eret
erit	er
et	e, et
Eulalia	Eulalia

F, f

Latin	Old French
facere	faire
faciam	fazet
figura	figure
focus	fou

A Brief History of Latin and Romance Languages Latin to Old French

Latin	Old French
fracture	fraint
frater	fradra, fradre
fuerit	furet
fugere	fuiet
fuit	fut

G, g

Latin	Old French
grandis	grand

H, h

Latin	Old French
habebat	auret
habet	auret
habuisset	avuisset
hoc	o
hominus	om
honestus	honestet

I, i

Latin	Old French
iectare	getterent
illa	elle, la, la, la, lei, li
illa-inde	ell'ent
ille	il, la, les, li, li, lo, lui
ille-inter	l'int
illi	les
illo	lo
illos	o's
impedimentum	empedementz
in	a, en, in, in, o
inhortor	enortet
in-ille	enl
inimicos	enimi
inter	int
intus	enz
iurat	iurat

L, l

Latin	Old French
laxare	laist, lazsier
lo	lo

Latin	Old French
Ludovicus	Lodhuuigs, Lodhuuuig, Ludher

M, m

Latin	Old French
malum	mals
Maximianus	Maximiien
me	me
meliorem	melz
merces	mercit
meum	meon
meus	meos
mihi	mi
minacia	manatce
ministerium	menestier
mortuus	mort, morte

N, n

Latin	Old French
nec	ne, ne, ned
nihil	niule
nomen	nom
non	ne, non, nun
non-se	no's
non-volet	no'nt
nostrum	nos, nostro
nullus	neuls, nul, nulla
nunquam	nonque, nunquam

O, o

Latin	Old French
orare	oram

P, p

Latin	Old French
pagani	pagiens
paganus	pagiens
paramentum	paramenz
pars	part
per	par, per
perdere	perdesse
placitum	plaid

A Brief History of Latin and Romance Languages — Latin to Old French

Latin	Old French
plicare	pleier
populum	poblo
possum	pois, pouret
post	post
potentem	podir
praesentem	presentede
precari	preier
precaria	preiement
prendere	prindrai
pro	por, Pro
puella	polle, pulcella

Q, q

Latin	Old French
quam-illa	qu'elle
quanto	quant
que	que, qui
qui	chi, cui
quid	que, qued, qued, quid
qui-illa	qu'elle

R, r

Latin	Old French
regalis	regiel
remanent	maent
reneget	raneiet
re-torno	returnar
rex	rex
rogare	roveret, ruovet

S, s

Latin	Old French
sacramentum	sagrament
salvamentum	saluar
salvare	saluarai
salvationem	saluament
sapere	sauir
semper	sempre
seniorem	sendra
servare	seruir
si	si, si
sic	si
sit	sit

Latin	Old French
solum	seule
spatha	spede
subtus	sus
super	soure
sustinere	sostendreiet
suum	souue, suon
suus	sa, son, suo

T, t

Latin	Old French
tantum-tostum	tantost
tolio	tolir
totus	tuit

U, u

Latin	Old French
unum	une
unumque	omque

V, v

Latin	Old French
venire	venir
vincere	veintre
virginitatem	virginitet
volare	volat
volat	volt
volere	voldret
voluerunt	voldrent
voluntatem	uol

Latin to Old Galician-Portuguese

Latin	Old Galician-Portuguese

A, a

a	a, a
ad	a
anima	alm'
auctoricare	outorgaría
audere	ousadía

B, b

bene	ben

C, c

carraria	carreira
credere	creer
cupla	culpados

D, d

dare	dar, dar-, daría
de	da, de, do
debere	devería, deves
demonstrare-nos	móstra-nos
Deus	Déus
diem	día

E, e

e	e
ego	e
erratus	errados
est	é
et	e

F, f

Latin	Old Galician-Portuguese
facere-illos	faze-los
faciem	fazer, fazía
follis	folía
foran	foran
fuisse	foss'

G, g

ganare	gãar
gaudia	goi'

I, i

ille	el, o
illos	lles
in	en
intendere	entender
iste	esta

L, l

laudare	loor
lux	luz

M, m

magis	mais
manuaria	maneira
Maria	María
mea	mía
monstrare	amostrar-
multum	mui

N, n

non	non
nos	nos

A Brief History of Latin and Romance Languages

Latin	Old Galician-Portuguese

P, p

Latin	Old Galician-Portuguese
paradisum	paraíso
parallelus	par
peccatum	pecados
per	per, per, pera, pera, por, pora
perdere	perder
perdonare	perdõados
placere	prazer-m-ía, prazía
posse	pód', pódes

Q, q

Latin	Old Galician-Portuguese
quaero	querría, quiso
quem	quen
qui	que, que, que, que
quia	ca

R, r

Latin	Old Galician-Portuguese
res-nata	ren
risus	riso

S, s

Latin	Old Galician-Portuguese
Sancta	Santa
semper	sempre
sensus	siso
si	se
sine	sen
singularis	senlleira
stella	strela
sunt	son, son

T, t

Latin	Old Galician-Portuguese
talis	tal
te	te, ti, ti, tu
tenere	ten
totus	toda

Latin to Old Galician-Portuguese

Latin	Old Galician-Portuguese
tui	téu

U, u

Latin	Old Galician-Portuguese
ubi	u

V, v

Latin	Old Galician-Portuguese
veritatem	verdadeira
via	vía
videre	veer

Latin to Old Italian

Latin	Old Italian
A, a	
a	a
ab	ab
ad	ad
aerem	aere
agros	pratalia
album	alba, albo
altissimus	altissimo, altissimu
amor	amore
anni	anni
aqua	aqua
arabat	araba
B, b	
beati	beati
bellus	belle, bello, bellu
Benedictus	Benedicti
benedire	benedicete, benedictione
bonus	bon
bovis	boves
bucca	boce
C, c	
caelus	celu
castus	casta
claritate	clarite
color	coloriti
confinis	konfàno
continere	contene
corporalem	corporale
creatura	creature
cum	con, cum
D, d	
dare	dài
de	da, de
dicere	dicere
dignus	dignu
diurnus	iorno
diversus	diversi
E, e	
e	e
eae	se
eccum ille	quelli
eccum-illa	kella, kelle
erunt	sirano
esse	si', sie
est	è, ène
et	et
excappare	scappare
F, f	
fero	farrà
finis	fini
florae	flori
focus	focu
formare	formate
forte	forte
frater	frate
fructus	fructi
G, g	
gloria	gloria
grande	grande
gratia	ringratiate
gubernare	governa
H, h	
herba	herba

Latin	Old Italian	Latin	Old Italian
homo	homo	*nigrum*	negro
honor	honore	*noctem*	nocte
humile	humile	*non*	no, non
humilitas	humilitate	*nos*	noi
		nostra	nostra
		nubilo	nubilo
		nullus	nullu

I, i

O, o

Latin	Old Italian	Latin	Old Italian
illa	la	*omne*	onne
ille	ello, ellu, l, le	*omnipotentem*	onnipotente
illui	lui		
in	in		
incoronare	incoronati		
inde	ne		
infirmitas	infirmitate		
in-foro	foro		
iucundus	iocundo		

P, p

L, l

Latin	Old Italian	Latin	Old Italian
laudat	laude	*parere*	pareba
laudate	laudate	*partum*	parte
laudato	laudato	*pax*	pace
lo	lo	*peccatum*	peccata
luminis	allumini, ennallumini	*per*	per
luna	luna	*perdonare*	perdonano
		Pergoaldus	Pergoaldi
		portare	porta
		possessio	posset, possette
		potest	pò
		pretiosus	pretiosa, pretiose
		productus	produce

M, m

Q, q

Latin	Old Italian	Latin	Old Italian
male	male	*qua*	ka
Maria	Marie	*quale*	quale
mater	matre	*qualis*	qual
mente habere	mentovare	*que*	que
messor	messor	*qui*	che, ki
mi	mi	*quia*	ca
monstrum	monstrai, mostrai	*quo*	ke, ko
morientur	morrano	*quod*	cco
mortalem	mortali		
mortem	morte		
multo	multo		

N, n

R, r

Latin	Old Italian
radians	radiante

Latin	Old Italian
robustus	robustoso

S, s

Latin	Old Italian
Sancta	sancte, Sancti
sanctissime	santissime
scio	sao
se	se
secreta	secrita
secundus	secunda
semen	semen
seminabat	seminaba
seniorem	signore
serenus	sereno
servare	serviateli
si	si
significatio	significatione
sol	sole
solus	solo
soror	sor, sora
specialis	spetialmente
splendor	splendore
stella	stelle
sunt	so
sustinere	sostengo, sosterrano, sustenta, sustentamento

T, t

Latin	Old Italian
te	te
te habes	l'ài
tempus	tempo
tenebat	teneba
terra	terra, terre
those	ille
tibi	tebe
totus	tucte
tribulatio	tribulatione
triginta	trenta
tropare	trovarà
tu	tue
tuum	tue, tuo

U, u

Latin	Old Italian
utile	utile

V, v

Latin	Old Italian
vae	guai
venti	vento
versorium	versorio
vivens	vivente
vobis	bobe
voluntas	voluntati

Latin to Old Occitan

Latin	Old Occitan

A, a

Latin	Old Occitan
a	a, a
ab	ab, ab
abuisset	l'agues
abuit	n'ac
ac sic	enaissi
ad	a, ad, al
ad-facere	afar
ad-hicce	aici
ad-pressum	apres
advenire	avinens
aestas	estat
alterum	autres
andare	anava
appellare	apellatz, appellatz
apprendere	aprendia
apud	ab
Arvernia	d'Alvernhe, d'Alvernhe
audire	l'auzir
audit	n'auzi

B, b

Latin	Old Occitan
baronem	barons
bassus	bas
bellus	bels
bene	ben
blasphemare	blasmava
Blavia	Blaia
bonum	bona
bonus	bons
bracchium	bratz
brevis	breus

C, c

Latin	Old Occitan
cantare	chanta
cantat	cantet
cantaverunt	cantavon
cantio	chansos
cantionem	canson, cansos, chantars, chantars
cantiones	chansos
cantores	cantadors
castellum	castel
clarificare	esclarzis
Clarus Mons	Clarmon
comitessa	comtessa
conductus	condug
cortem	cortz
crux	croset
cum	con

D, d

Latin	Old Occitan
dabat	dava
dalphinus	Dalfins
de	de, del
de ille	del
de unum	d'un
de-amor	d'amor
debere	denan
de-eccum-ille	d'aquels
de-illos	dels
de-iste	dis
de-juxta	dejosta
de-subter	desotz
de-super	desobr'e
de-unde	on
de-unum	dun
Deus	Dieu
dicere	dis, ditz, ditz, ditz:
diem	dia
diurnum	jorns
dixit	dire
dolorem	dolor
dulce	dous
dunc	adoncs
duo	dos

A Brief History of Latin and Romance Languages — Latin to Old Occitan

Latin	Old Occitan

E, e

Latin	Old Occitan
ea	ella
ecclesia	eglesia, glesia
eccum ille	aquel
eccum-ille	aquels
eccum-talis	aitals
enamorat	enamoret
entro	tro
episcopus	l'evesquat
erant	eran
erat	era
essere	sei
est	es
et	ab, e, et, l'agues
et is	e.ls
Exidolium	d'Esiduoill

F, f

factum	faita
factus	faichs
fecit	fait, fetz, fetz, fez
filius	filhs
flagrare	flairar
fortis	fort
fuissent	fosson
fuisset	fos
fuit	fo, foron

G, g

gens	gen
gentilis	gentils
Gervasius	Gervas
Giraudus	Girautz, Guirautz
grand	gran
grandis	gran
gratitus	grasitz

H, h

habebat	l'avia
habet	a, avia
hibernus	l'invern
hominem	hom, hom, om
homines	homes
honoratus	honratz, onratz
honorem	honor
him	se

I, i

illa	la
ille	e.l, e·l, el, el, lui;
illeius	leis
illos	als
illu	lo, lo, lo, lo
illui	lui
in	en, en
in-hanc-horam	anc, anc, ancar, ancaras
intellegentem	enten
intendere	entendenz, entendon
inter	entre
intro	antre
is	es, is
is-erat	estava

J, j

| Jaufredus | Jaufres |

L, l

laudat	lausava, lauzet
lectuo	leit
Lemovicinus	Lemoges, Limozi
littera	letras
litteras	letras
litteratus	letratz
longa-mente	longamen
longue	loncs

A Brief History of Latin and Romance Languages   Latin to Old Occitan

Latin	Old Occitan
M, m	
magis	ma
magistralis	maestrals
male habitus	malautia
mansionem	maison
manus tenir ant	mantenent
mare	mar
meliorem	meilhor, meilhors, meiller
meum	mon
minare	menava
misit	mes
monacha	morga
mons	mon
mors	mort
mortuus	mori
mulierem	muiller
multi	mains
multum	mout
mundum	mon
muttum	motz
N, n	
naturalem	natural
navem	nau
nec	ni, ni
nec-unus	neguna
nominem	nom
non	no
not	non
non-venit-magis	mais
nullus	nulls
P, p	
paenitentia	penedensa
parentem	parenz
pauculum	pauc
pauper	paubres
per	per, per, per
peregrinus	pelerins

Latin	Old Occitan
persona	persona
Petrus	Peire
placere	plazen
poena	penas
poeta	pauzatz
posse	pois
possum	pois, puois, puois
poveres	paubres
prendere	pres, pres
primus	primieira, primiers
principe	princes
Q, q	
qua-illos	quals
quam-erunt	qu'eron
qui	qe, que, que
quia	qu'a
quid	que
qui-intendere	qu'entendian
qui-me	que.m
qui-unum	qu'un
quod ella	qu'el, qu'el, qu'ella, qu'ella
R, r	
recuperare	recobret
regio-incontrata	l'encontrada
rem	ren
rendere	rendet
S, s	
Sanctus	Saint
sapere	saber, saup, savis
sapiens	savis
scholam	escola
scriptum	escritas
se	se, se, se, se
secondum	segon
se-illos	soas
se-illus	sieus

Latin	Old Occitan	Latin	Old Occitan
sepulcrum	sepellir	vox	votz
so	si, so		
si	so		
sic	si, si:		
sine	ses		
sonorem	sons		
status	estat		
stetit	estet		
sua	soa		
subtilis	subtils		
sunt	son		
suos	soas		
sustinere	sostenguda, tengutz		
suum	son, sos		
suus	soas, son, sos		

T, t

Latin	Old Occitan
talem	tal
Templum	Temple
tempus	temps
totus	tot, tota, totas, totz, toz

U, u

Latin	Old Occitan
ultra	outra
unum	un

V, v

Latin	Old Occitan
valere	valens
venit	venc, venguen
versum	vers
vespers	sers
vicecomes	viscomte
videre	vezer, vezer
villa	villa
vista	vista
vita	vida
vivere	visquet
voluit	volc
voluntat	voluntat

Old French to English

Old French	English

A, a

Old French	English
a	in, in, to
ab	with
ad	to
adiudha	aid
adunet	worships
aiudha	aid
altresi	likewise
amast	to-love
amur	the-love-of
anima	soul
arde	burn
argent	silver
auant	future
auret	had, had
avuisset	may-have

B, b

Old French	English
bel	graceful
bellezour	beautiful
buona	good

C, c

Old French	English
cadhuna	every
celle	this
cels	those
chi	who
chieef	head
chielt	was-bothered
christian	christian
christiien	Christian (name)
Christus	Christ (name)
ciel	heaven
cist	to-this
clementia	clemency
coist	burn
colomb	a-dove
colpes	sin
com	with
commun	common
concreidre	to-believe
conselliers	counsellers
conservat	keeps
contra	against
contredist	oppose
corps	body
cosa	thing
cose	thing
cui	who
cum	as
czo	this

D, d

Old French	English
damno	damnation
de	of
degnet	worthy
Deo	God (name), God (name)
Deus	God (name)
di	day
diaule	the-devil
dis	days
dist	should
d'ist	of-this
domnizelle	damsel
dont	but-then
dreit	right
dunat	gives

E, e

Old French	English
e	and
element	god
elle	she
ell'ent	she-then
empedementz	persecution
en	in

A Brief History of Latin and Romance Languages — Old French to English

Old French	English
enimi	enemies
enl	in-the
enortet	encourages
enz	inside
eo	I
er	will-be
eret	was
eskoltet	listen
et	and
Eulalia	Eulalia (name)

F, f

Old French	English
faire	do
fazet	shall-do
figure	the-figure
fou	fire
fradra	brother
fradre	brother
fraint	breaks
fuiet	flee
furet	she-would
fut	was

G, g

Old French	English
getterent	they-threw
grand	grand

H, h

Old French	English
honestet	honour

I, i

Old French	English
il	he
in	in, in-to
int	him-from
io	I
iurat	sworn

J, j

Old French	English
ju	I

K, k

Old French	English
Karle	Charles (name)
Karlo	Charles (name)
Karlus	Charles (name)
kose	thing
Krist	Christ (name)

L, l

Old French	English
la	her, she, the, the
laist	allow
lazsier	to-leave
lei	she
les	the, the
li	her, the, to-him
l'int	him-from
lo	it, the, the
Lodhuuigs	Louis (name)
Lodhuuuig	Louis (name)
Ludher	Lothair (name)
lui	him

M, m

Old French	English
maent	resides
mals	evil
manatce	threats
Maximiien	Maximian (name)
me	me
melz	better
menestier	service
meon	my
meos	mine
mercit	mercy
mi	to-me
mort	death
morte	die

A Brief History of Latin and Romance Languages   Old French to English

Old French	English

N, n

Old French	English
ne	neither, nor, not
ned	neither
neuls	no-one
niule	nothing
nom	name
non	not
nonque	never
no'nt	did-not-want
nos	our
no's	did-not
nostro	our
nul	not
nulla	no
nun	not
nunquam	never

O, o

Old French	English
o	in-so-far-as, this
om	a-man
omque	once
or	gold
oram	to-pray
o's	this

P, p

Old French	English
pagiens	of-the-pagans, the-pagans
par	by
paramenz	adornments
part	part
per	by
perdesse	lose
plaid	council
pleier	bend
poblo	the-people
podir	power
pois	am-able
polle	girl

Old French	English
por	for
post	after
pouret	able
preiement	prayers
preier	to-pray-for
presentede	presented
prindrai	shall-take
Pro	for
pulcella	girl

Q, q

Old French	English
quant	how-much
que	that, which
qued	that, which
qu'elle	than-she, which-she
qui	which
quid	that

R, r

Old French	English
raneiet	deny
regiel	regal
returnar	dissuade
rex	king
roveret	order
ruovet	calls-for

S, s

Old French	English
sa	her
sagrament	sacrament
saluament	salvation
saluar	to-protect
saluarai	will-protect
sauir	wisdom
sempre	always
sendra	lord
seruir	serve
seule	earthly-life
si	if, so, thus
sit	may-be
son	his

Old French	English
sostendreiet	she-would-undergo
soure	over
souue	his
spede	sword
suo	his
suon	his
sus	up

T, t

tantost	so-quickly
tolir	take-off
tuit	all

U, u

une	a
uol	will

V, v

veintre	kill
venir	to-come
virginitet	virginity
volat	to-fly
voldrent	wanted
voldret	want
volt	she-wants

Old Galician-Portuguese to English

Old Galician-Portuguese	English
A, a	
a	of, that, to
alm'	soul
amostrar-	show
B, b	
ben	well
C, c	
ca	because
carreira	the-path
companñía	company
creer	believe
culpados	guilty
D, d	
da	for
dar	give
dar-	give
daría	giving
de	of
Déus	God (name)
devería	should
deves	you-must
día	day
do	of
E, e	
e	and, I, of
el	him
en	in
entender	understand
errados	mistaken
esta	this
É, é	
é	is
F, f	
faze-los	make-those
fazer	made
fazía	made
folía	reckless
foran	they-were
foss'	to-have-been
G, g	
gãar	to-win
goi'	joy
guía	guide
guïar	guide
L, l	
lles	them
loor	praise
luz	light
M, m	
mais	but
maneira	deeds
María	Maria (name)
mía	my
móstra-nos	show-us
mui	very

A Brief History of Latin and Romance Languages

Old Galician-Portuguese	English

N, n

| non | not |
| nos | us |

O, o

o	the
ousadía	boldness
outorgaría	bestow

P, p

par	match
paraíso	paradise
pecados	sin
per	because-of, by
pera	because, to
perder	lost
perdõados	pardoned
pód'	can
pódes	can
por	for
pora	for
prazer-m-ía	should-rejoice
prazía	pleases

Q, q

que	that, what, which, who
quen	whoever
querría	willingly
quiso	seeks

R, r

| ren | nothing |
| riso | delight |

S, s

Old Galician-Portuguese to English

Old Galician-Portuguese	English
Santa	Saint (name)
se	if
sempre	always
sen	without
senlleira	singularly
siso	sense
son	they, they-are
strela	star

T, t

tal	such
te	you
ten	has
téu	of-you
ti	you, your
toda	all
tu	you

U, u

| u | where |

V, v

veer	to-see
verdadeira	truth
vía	the-way

Old Italian to English

Old Italian	English

A, a

a	is, to
ab	out-of
ad	to
aere	the-air
alba	white
albo	a-white
allumini	the-light
altissimo	the-highest
altissimu	the-highest
amore	love
anni	years
aqua	water
araba	he-plowed

B, b

beati	blessed
belle	beautiful
bello	handsome
bellu	beautiful
benedicete	bless
Benedicti	Benedict (name)
benedictione	blessing
bobe	to-you
boce	the-mouth
bon	good
boves	oxen

C, c

ca	as
casta	pure
cco	that
celu	heaven
che	who
clarite	clearly
coloriti	coloured
con	with
contene	contained
corporale	of-the-body
creature	creatures
cum	with

D, d

da	from, of
dài	given
de	of
dicere	to-speak
dignu	worthy
diversi	diverse

E, e

e	and
ello	he
ellu	he
ennallumini	illuminates
et	and

F, f

farrà	bring
fini	borders
flori	flowers
focu	fire
formate	formed
foro	by-the-court
forte	strong
frate	brother
fructi	fruits

G, g

gloria	glory
governa	maintains
grande	grand

A Brief History of Latin and Romance Languages   Old Italian to English

Old Italian	English
guai	woe

H, h

Old Italian	English
herba	herbs
homo	man
honore	honour
humile	humble
humilitate	humility

I, i

ille	the
in	in
incoronati	crowned
infirmitate	infirmity
iocundo	playful
iorno	the-day

K, k

ka	that
ke	who
kella	this
kelle	these
ki	here, who
ko	that
konfàno	belong

L, l

l	the
la	the, this
l'ài	you-have
laudate	praise
laudato	praise
laude	praises
le	the
lo	is, the, this
lui	him
luna	moon

M, m

Old Italian	English
male	harm
Marie	Mary (name)
matre	mother
mentovare	mentioning
messor	the-harvester
mi	my
monstrai	demonstrated
morrano	die
mortali	mortal
morte	death
mostrai	demonstrated
multo	much

N, n

ne	us, while
negro	black
no	not
nocte	night
noi	ours
non	not
nostra	ours
nubilo	the-clouds
nullu	no

O, o

onne	all, every
onnipotente	almighty

P, p

pace	peace
pareba	led
parte	acquired
peccata	sin
per	because-of, by, through
perdonano	pardon
Pergoaldi	Pergoaldo (name)

A Brief History of Latin and Romance Languages — Old Italian to English

Old Italian	English
pò	may
porta	brings
posset	possession
possette	possession
pratalia	fields
pretiosa	precious
pretiose	preciously
produce	produces

Q, q

Old Italian	English
qual	which
quale	which
que	that
quelli	those

R, r

Old Italian	English
radiante	radiant
ringratiate	give-thanks
robustoso	robust

S, s

Old Italian	English
sancte	Saint (name)
Sancti	Saint (name)
santissime	sacred
sao	I-know
scappare	escape
se	he, they
secrita	secrets
secunda	following
semen	seed
seminaba	he-sowed
sereno	serene
serviateli	serve
si	be
si'	be
sie	be
significatione	signification
signore	lord
sirano	they-will-be
so	are

Old Italian	English
sole	sun
solo	alone
sor	sister
sora	sister
sostengo	endure
sosterrano	endure
spetialmente	especially
splendore	splendour
stelle	stars
sustenta	sustains
sustentamento	sustenance

T, t

Old Italian	English
te	you
tebe	to-you
tempo	weather
teneba	he-held
terra	earth, land
terre	lands
trenta	thirty
tribulatione	tribulation
trovarà	find
tucte	all
tue	you, your, yours
tuo	your

U, u

Old Italian	English
utile	useful

V, v

Old Italian	English
vento	wind
versorio	plough
vivente	living
voluntati	will

Old Occitan to English

Old Occitan	English

A, a

a	a, has, of, to
ab	and, from, if, with
ad	to
adoncs	of-once
afar	affairs
aici	here
aitals	such
al	to
alberc	inn
als	by
anava	he-went
anc	ever, still
ancar	still
ancaras	still
antre	into
apellatz	was-called
appellatz	was-called
aprendia	learning
apres	after
aquel	that-very
aquels	anyone
autres	others
avia	has
avinens	comely

B, b

barons	barons
bas	low
bels	beautiful
ben	good, well
Blaia	Blaye (place)
blasmava	blamed
bona	good
bons	good
borges	burgher
Borneilh	Bourney (place)
Borneill	Bourney (place)
Bornelh	Bornelh (place)
bratz	arms
breus	short

C, c

canson	song
cansos	songs
cantadors	singers
cantavon	sang
cantet	sang
castel	castle
chansos	songs, songs
chanta	singing
chantars	song, songs
Clarmon	Clermont
comtessa	countess
con	with
condug	taken
cortz	court
croset	the-cross

D, d

d'Antiocha	Antioch (place)
Dalfins	Dauphin
d'Alvernhe	d'Alvernhe, of-Auvergne
d'amor	of-love
d'aquels	of-anyone
dava	he-gave
de	of, of
dejosta	of-while
del	of, of
dels	of-the
denan	before
d'Esiduoill	Excideuil (place)
desobr'e	above-or
desotz	below
dia	day
Dieu	God (name)
dire	said

Old Occitan	English
dis	this, told
ditz	sayings, words
ditz:	says
dolor	pain
dompnas	ladies
dos	two
dous	before
dun	of
d'un	of-a

E, e

Old Occitan	English
e	and
e.l	his
e.ls	and-the
e·l	his
eglesia	church
el	he, him
ella	she
en	in, on
enaissi	thus
enamoret	enamoured
enten	understand
entendenz	understood
entendon	understand
entre	in
era	was
eran	at-that-time
es	he, is
esclarzis	he-clarify
escola	school
escritas	written
estat	existed, summer
estava	he-was
estet	stayed
et	and

F, f

Old Occitan	English
faichs	made
fait	made
faita	made
fetz	did, made
fez	made

Old Occitan	English
filhs	son
flairar	smell
fo	was
foron	was
fort	strongly
fos	was
fosson	had-been-made

G, g

Old Occitan	English
gazaingnava	earned
gen	gentle
gentils	noble
Gervas	Gervaise (name)
Girautz	Giraut (name)
glesia	church
gran	grand, grand
grasitz	favoured
Guirautz	Giraut (name)

H, h

Old Occitan	English
hom	a-man, man
homes	men
honor	honour
honratz	honoured

I, i

Old Occitan	English
is	the

J, j

Old Occitan	English
Jaufres	Jaufré (name)
jorns	days

L, l

Old Occitan	English
l'agues	had
l'auzir	hearing
l'avia	he-had

A Brief History of Latin and Romance Languages Old Occitan to English

Old Occitan	English
la	the
las	those
lausava	praised
lauzet	praised
leis	her
leit	bedside
Lemoges	Limoges (place)
l'encontrada	region-encountered
letras	letters, letters
letratz	letters
l'evesquat	bishop
Limozi	Limoges (place)
l'invern	the-winter
lo	a, had, him, the
loncs	long
longamen	long
los	those
lui	him
lui;	him

M, m

Old Occitan	English
ma	but
maestrals	masterful
maestre	master
mains	many
mais	never
maison	house
malautia	sickness
mantenent	now
mar	the-sea
mas	but
meilhor	better
meilhors	best
meiller	better
menava	lead
mes	see-out
mon	me, mountains, the-world
morga	a-nun
mori	died
mort	death
motz	words
mout	very
muiller	a-wife

N, n

Old Occitan	English
n'ac	with-loss
n'auzi	he-heard
nasquet	was-born
natural	natural
nau	ship
neguna	not-one
negus	nor-any
ni	either, or
no	not
nom	name
non	not
nulls	no

O, o

Old Occitan	English
om	man
on	in
onratz	honoured
outra	beyond

P, p

Old Occitan	English
parenz	parents
paubres	poor, simple
pauc	little
pauzatz	poetise
Peire	Peire (name)
pelerins	pilgrims
penas	unfortunately
penedensa	penance
per	because, by, near
persona	persona
plazen	praise
pois	could-be, then
pres	fell, took
primieira	first
primiers	first
princes	prince
puois	could, then

A Brief History of Latin and Romance Languages   Old Occitan to English

Old Occitan	English
Q, q	
qe	which
qu'el	that-her, which
qu'ella	that-she, which-she
qu'a	which
quals	of-which
que	than, that, when, which, which, who
que.m	who-me
qu'el	which
qu'entendian	who-understood
qu'eron	who-were
qu'un	that-a
R, r	
recobret	recovered
ren	things
rendet	became
ric	rich
Rudels	Rudel (name)
S, s	
saber	known
Saint	Saint (name)
saup	understood
savis	clever, clever
se	him, himself, took, was, went
segon	according-to
sei	you-are
sen	sense
sepellir	buried
sers	evenings
ses	without
si	so, so
si:	this
sieus	his
so	so, so
soa	his
soas	his, his, his

Old Occitan	English
son	his, his, yourself
sons	sounds
sos	her, his
sostenguda	sustained
subtils	subtle
T, t	
tal	such
Temple	Temple (place)
temps	time
tengutz	sustained
tot	all
tota	all
totas	all
totz	all
toz	all
Tripol	Tripoli (place)
tro	until
trobador	troubadour
trobadors	troubadours
trobaire	troubadour
trobet	composed-poetry
U, u	
un	an
V, v	
valens	valiant
valenz	valiant
venc	came
venguen	came-from
vers	verses
vezer	seeing, to-see
vida	life
villa	city
viscomte	viscount
visquet	lived
vista	seen
volc	wanted
voluntat	he-longed

Old Occitan	English
votz	voice